GCSE

David Faithfull
Chris Newbould
David Swinscoe

Text © Chris Newbould, David Faithfull and David Swinscoe 2009
Original illustrations © Nelson Thornes Ltd 2009

The right of Chris Newbould, David Faithfull and David Swinscoe to be identified as authors of this work has been asserted by them in accordance with the Copyright, Designs and Patents Act 1988.

All rights reserved. No part of this publication may be reproduced or transmitted in any form or by any means, electronic or mechanical, including photocopy, recording or any information storage and retrieval system, without permission in writing from the publisher or under licence from the Copyright Licensing Agency Limited, of Saffron House, 6–10 Kirby Street, London, EC1N 8TS.

Any person who commits any unauthorised act in relation to this publication may be liable to criminal prosecution and civil claims for damages.

Published in 2009 by:
Nelson Thornes Ltd
Delta Place
27 Bath Road
CHELTENHAM
GL53 7TH
United Kingdom

09 10 11 12 13 / 10 9 8 7 6 5 4 3 2 1

A catalogue record for this book is available from the British Library

ISBN 978 1 4085 0397 3

Cover photograph: Bronwyn Fecteau

The authors and publisher would like to thank Ambrose Chan and Alex Mitchell, students of Tonbridge School, for posing for the cover photograph.

Page make-up and illustrations by Tech-Set Ltd, Gateshead

Printed and bound in Spain by GraphyCems

Photograph Acknowledgements

The authors and publisher are grateful to the following for permission to reproduce photographs and other copyright material in this book.

Chris Newbould: C3, 3.1F, 11.2A, 11.2C, 11.2K, C12, 12.2C, 14.5A; **David Faithfull**: C2, 2.1A, C5, 5.1B, 5.2A, 6.1A, 6.1B, 6.1E, 6.1F, 6.1G, C7, 7.4A, 7.4C, 7.4D, C9, 9.2A, 9.3A, 9.3C, 9.6A; **David Swinscoe**: C4, 4.1C, 4.1D, 4.1E, 4.1F, 4.1G, 4.2H, C10, 10.1B, 10.1F; **Fotolia**: C1, 1.1A , 1.3C, 8.1D, C13, 13.2B, 13.2D; **iStockphoto**: C8, 8.1B, C11, C14.

Every effort has been made to trace and contact all copyright holders and we apologise if any have been overlooked. The publisher will be pleased to make the necessary arrangements at the first opportunity.

Contents

Introduction ... 5

1 Electrical safety ... 8
1.1 Dangers of electricity ... 8
1.2 Mains circuits ... 10
1.3 Prevention of accidents ... 11

2 Real electronic systems ... 14
2.1 What exactly is a system? ... 14
2.2 Identifying the inputs and outputs of the system ... 15
2.3 Designing systems ... 18

3 Building and testing a simple system ... 21
3.1 Basic equipment ... 21
3.2 Resistors ... 24
3.3 Light-emitting diodes (LEDs) ... 27

4 Decision making circuits ... 30
4.1 Switches ... 30
4.2 Logic gates ... 32

5 Boosting the signal ... 38
5.1 Transducer drivers using transistors ... 38
5.2 Transducer drivers using relay switches ... 42

6 Making time delays ... 46
6.1 Capacitors ... 46
6.2 Time delay circuits ... 50

7 Making continuous pulses ... 54
7.1 Uses of continuous pulses ... 54
7.2 Generating the signal ... 55
7.3 Making the pulses ... 56
7.4 Checking for a pulse ... 59

8 Latching and counting circuits ... 65
8.1 Counting circuits ... 65
8.2 Latches and frequency dividers ... 69

Contents

9 Comparing signals — 73
- 9.1 Introducing comparator circuits — 73
- 9.2 The operational amplifier — 74
- 9.3 Sensing the light — 77
- 9.4 The voltage divider — 78
- 9.5 The porch light circuit — 80
- 9.6 Sensing other things — 81

10 Audio systems — 84
- 10.1 What is an audio system? — 84

11 Power supplies — 87
- 11.1 What is mains ac? — 87
- 11.2 Why do we need to convert to dc? — 88

12 Radio systems — 93
- 12.1 Radio communication — 93
- 12.2 A simple radio receiver — 95
- 12.3 AM and FM transmissions — 97

13 Programmed systems — 100
- 13.1 Microcontrollers — 100
- 13.2 Converting between analogue and digital signals — 101
- 13.3 Flowchart diagrams — 102

14 The Controlled Assessment — 104
- 14.1 Introducing the Controlled Assessment — 104
- 14.2 Getting to grips with design — 105
- 14.3 Planning — 107
- 14.4 Can I get started? — 110
- 14.5 The written report — 112

Examination-style questions — 113
Answers to summary questions — 122
Useful information for GCSE Electronics — 123
Glossary — 125
Index — 127

Nelson Thornes and AQA

Nelson Thornes has worked in partnership with AQA to make sure that this book offers you the best possible support for your GCSE course. All the content has been approved by the senior examining team at AQA, so you can be sure that it gives you just what you need when you are preparing for your exams.

How to use this book

This book covers everything you need for your course.

Learning objectives

At the beginning of each section or topic you'll find a list of Learning Objectives based on the requirements of the specification, so you can make sure you are covering everything you need to know for the exam.

AQA Examiner's tips

Don't forget to look at the AQA Examiner's Tips throughout the book to help you with your study and prepare for your exam.

AQA Examiner's tip

Don't forget to look at the AQA Examiner's tips throughout the book to help you with your study and prepare for your exam.

AQA Examination-style questions

These offer opportunities to practise doing questions in the style that you can expect in your exam so that you can be fully prepared on the day.

AQA examination questions are reproduced by permission of the Assessment and Qualifications Alliance.

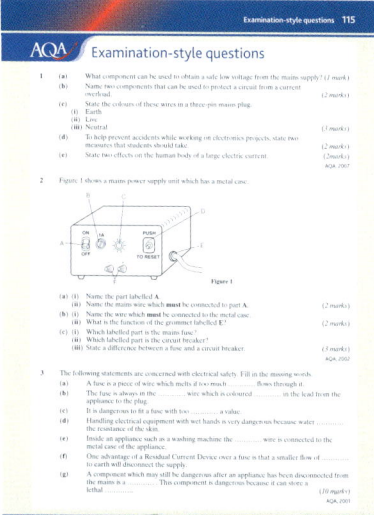

Visit **www.nelsonthornes.com/aqagcse** for more information.

Introduction

Studying GCSE Electronics

Electronics is an engineering subject, which means it is about designing and making useful things to solve problems. Studying Electronics can improve your skills in many areas. It is important to get the right balance between practising the theory and mathematics involved in Electronics, and practical work and activities.

Aim of the student book

This book is designed to support the new AQA GCSE Electronics specification. It will help you understand the science of electronics and is also a good starting point for anyone wanting to learn electronics. The material is arranged in a logical working order but it may be the case that your teacher chooses to mix this up a bit. Throughout the book you will find link boxes to direct you to other places in the book where topics have been covered.

Practice makes perfect!

The book is full of circuits for you to build. You will find building these circuits not only develops your practical skills but also helps you understand the ideas. You should put together as many circuits as you can to test your understanding and try out your ideas. Try to be neat and logical when laying out your circuits. It will save you time in the long run and make the ideas easier to understand.

There are lots of questions throughout the book for you to try. Practising questions will help you to understand the science involved. The answers to the questions are in the back of the book for you to check your work, but try not to look at the answer until you have attempted the question. If you find a question difficult try reading the relevant topic of the book and try again!

The Controlled Assessment

The book contains lots of questions and activities designed to help develop skills that will come in useful for the Controlled Assessment. There is also a dedicated Controlled Assessment chapter to give you the best chance of success.

Please note that the Controlled Assessment chapter is designed to help you prepare for that task. The smaller activities that you will find throughout the book are not designed to test you formally and you cannot use them as your own Controlled Assessment tasks for AQA. Your teacher will not be able to give you as much help with your tasks for AQA as we have given with some of the tasks in this book.

Equipment

The equipment needed for most of the activities in this book does not have to be expensive. All of the components are easily available and you can use batteries for power supplies. Some test equipment, like oscilloscopes, can be expensive but most testing can be done with a cheap digital multimeter. Most Science departments will already have access to the equipment you will need.

Power supplies

Throughout the book we have used 9 V as the power supply for the circuits. However, almost any voltage supply between 3 V and 15 V can be used, provided component values are adjusted accordingly (e.g. by using current limiting resistors).

Enjoy!

We hope that you will enjoy studying this course and doing the practical work. We believe that the skills and knowledge that you will gain from the course will set you apart and enable you to participate more confidently in a world that increasingly relies on this technology.

If you get on well with the subject, remember that it is designed to follow on to the AQA Electronics course at AS/A2.

1 Electrical safety

1.1 Dangers of electricity

What are the dangers?

Whenever there is a voltage present in a circuit then this can present a danger to the user. The voltage represents an energy level which will cause an electric current to flow to a place where the voltage is lower. Mains circuits use high voltages and this means you should be particularly careful!

Modern systems often contain a mixture of high and low voltage circuits. The high voltage circuit is needed to process the supply of power from the mains socket and converts it into the low voltage needed by the electronic circuits (see Chapter 11). In some applications the conversion from high to low voltage is done by an external circuit which you plug into the mains socket. For example, the charger used for a mobile phone. From a safety point of view, you should not be working on any circuit that has mains electricity coming directly onto the circuit board.

Dangers from low voltage dc circuits (0–30 V)

This voltage range should not be exceeded when you are working on projects. In most cases you will not need to exceed 15 V and your natural body resistance will allow you to handle the circuits safely. However, you should always be cautious as there may still be dangers from components and other circuit faults.

- **Burns:** When excess current flows through components due to a fault or poor circuit design, they may become hot and you can receive burns. In particular, you need to be careful with resistors and Integrated Circuits (ICs).
- **Explosions:** These can occur if too much voltage is applied across components such as light-emitting diodes (LEDs) and capacitors. The voltage specification for the components should not be exceeded.

Objectives

In this section you will learn:

how to identify where electrical dangers might be present as part of an overall risk assessment

about the effect of an electric current on the human body

the procedure for dealing with an electric shock victim.

A *Beware if you see this sign! It means electrical danger*

Activity

Using a good quality Digital Multimeter (DMM) set to the highest resistance range (greater than 2 MΩ), measure your skin resistance by holding the probes between your thumb and fingers of each hand. Try this with dry hands and then try again having wet your fingers first.

Dangers from high voltage ac circuits (230 V mains)

NEVER work on any mains circuit! It is far too dangerous. The energy available is sufficient to overcome your body resistance and may result in a fatal shock.

As well as the dangers associated with the low voltage circuits, additional dangers from high voltage circuits come from:

- **Fire/explosions:** These can be caused if sparks from switches or wiring faults ignite gases, liquids, sprays, powder or dust in the air around where you are working.
- **Stored charge:** This can leave a high voltage on capacitors even when the circuit is switched off and create sparks or give you an electrical shock.
- **Electric shock:** An *electric shock* occurs when your body receives sufficient energy from a high voltage source to create a conductive path through your body. The current seeks to run to a low voltage point, for example, the ground. Although factors such as your general health, moisture and skin condition can influence the overall effect of an electric shock, the main factors that influence its effect on your body are the size of the current and the time for which you are in contact with the source.

Table **B** shows how some typical currents flowing through the body from a mains ac supply can affect the body.

> **Key terms**
>
> **Electric shock:** the effect on nerves, organs and tissue due to the passage of electrical current through the body.
>
> **Fibrillation:** stimulation of the heart muscles that overrides the natural rhythm.

> **Hint**
>
> 1 mA is the abbreviation for 1 milliamp. This is equal to 1 thousandth of an amp.

B *The effects of different currents on the body*

Current	Effect on the body
1 mA	Maximum safe current.
10 mA	Muscular spasms: may not be able to let go of the wire.
100 mA	**Fibrillation** of the heart occurs which is likely to be fatal. Burns may also be seen where current enters/exits the body.

First aid

What to do in an emergency

If you are working in a laboratory and suspect that someone has suffered an electric shock, you should be able to offer basic help.

Know your environment

You should be able to:
- locate and use the telephone
- recall the procedure for contacting the emergency services
- describe where you are.

Know basic first aid procedures

Upon coming across a possible electric shock victim you should:
1. make the scene of the accident safe by isolating the mains / move body away from the mains supply using an insulating aid
2. summon help
3. assess the casualty using the basic first aid assessment procedure by checking **AIRWAY**, **BREATHING** and **CIRCULATION**
4. carry out resuscitation if the casualty has stopped breathing, but only if you have been trained in the technique.

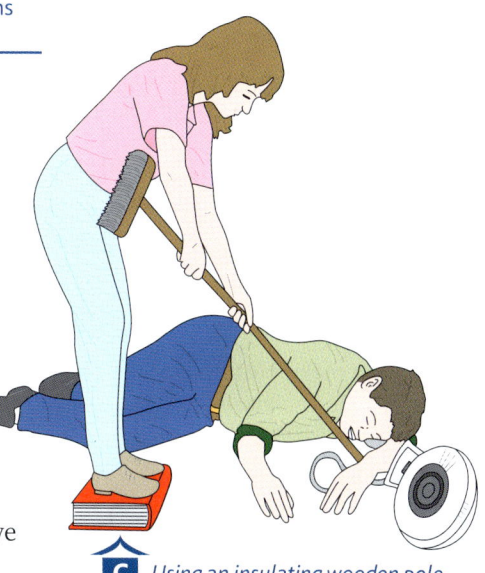

C *Using an insulating wooden pole to move the live wire away from the casualty*

1.2 Mains circuits

Most electrical accidents that occur in the home and in industry will be due to faults on mains circuits. It is therefore important to understand how to make your environment safe by not working alone, and to understand how the basic mains circuit works.

Circuits based upon transformers are used to obtain safe low voltages from the mains. Such low voltage supplies can then be used to power the electronic circuits found in many modern appliances.

Objectives

In this section you will learn:

how to wire a mains plug

the safety features of mains cabling.

links

You will learn about power supply circuits in Chapter 11.

■ Using mains cabling

A battery-powered circuit uses the traditional two wire system. One wire comes from the high energy end of the battery (+) and the other provides the return to the low energy end (−). However, due to the much higher energies that are found in the mains circuit, it has **three** wires of which one acts as a safety wire.

Depending on the amount of current expected to flow in the circuit, the cable can be obtained in different thicknesses. Using the correct size cable in an application avoids the generation of heat which may become a fire hazard. Using rubber grommets to feed mains cable through metal cases of an appliance avoids cuts to the cable.

The mains plug

Electrical appliances should be sold with a plug already in place; however, you may need to replace a plug later if it gets damaged.

- **LIVE** (brown): This wire is the high energy wire and drives the current backwards and forwards.
- **NEUTRAL** (blue): This wire is used to complete the circuit back to the source.
- **EARTH** (yellow and green stripes): This is the safety wire.

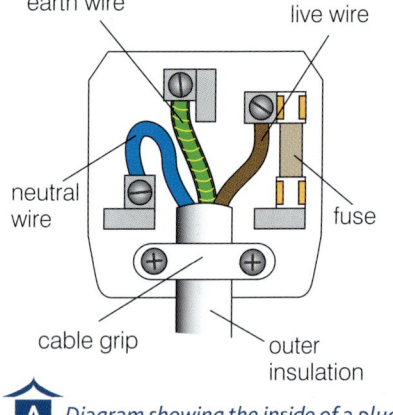

A Diagram showing the inside of a plug

Activity

Wire up a mains plug using three-core mains cable, making sure you check the following points:
- Wires should be in the correct terminals and secured firmly.
- Bare wire does not extend beyond the terminal as this can create a short circuit.
- There should be no cuts in the inner or outer insulated sheathing.
- The outer sheathing must be trapped under the cord grip to stop the individual wires being pulled out of the terminals.

LABORATORY SAFETY NOTE: The mains wire used for the exercise should be adequately insulated/terminated at the free end and it should not be possible to insert the plug into a live mains socket.

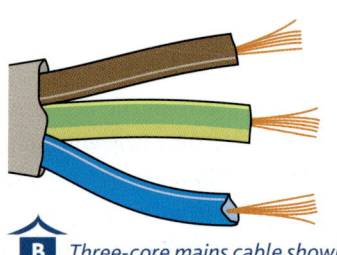

B Three-core mains cable showing the ends stripped ready to put into a plug

1.3 Prevention of accidents

■ Risk assessment

A risk assessment is just as it sounds – you need to assess the risks! A **risk assessment** involves identifying dangers associated with carrying out an activity, and taking the appropriate actions to reduce risk. As part of your risk assessment, you should be aware of the main dangers both from the low voltage electronic circuits you will be building and the high voltage mains circuits that are often used to bring power to those circuits in commercial applications.

The power supplies to all mains-operated portable appliances should be tested by a qualified engineer under the **PAT** legislation. Industry and education has a duty of care to employees and students to make sure that the environment in which they work (including the equipment that they use) is safe. Part of that safety check is to make sure that all portable appliances have been electrically tested. However, as a mark of good practice, you should be aware of the safety features and always carry out a visual check of the casing, wire and plug and report any damage you find.

■ Safety features in a mains electrical system

- The **fuse** is always placed in the live lead of the supply. It is designed to burn out and break the circuit if too much current flows. This should prevent damage to the appliance. The following electrical power equation is normally used to calculate the fuse value.

$$P = V \times I$$

where P is the electrical power in watts, V is the applied voltage in volts and I is the current flowing in amps.

- The fuse value must be selected so that it just exceeds the calculated current.

Example

A 2 kW hair dryer is to be used on a 230 V mains supply. What fuse should be used? Select from 1 A; 5 A; 10 A; 13 A.

Answer:
To find the current that flows through the fuse and the hair dryer, use the electrical power equation.

$$P = V = I$$

therefore

$$I = \frac{P}{V}$$

$$I = \frac{2000\,W}{230\,V}$$

$$I = 8.7\,A$$

The fuse that is most appropriate (next highest value) from the options available is the 10 A fuse.

- The earth lead provides a low resistance route from the metal case of any appliance to the ground. It is there to protect the user should any fault develop that might cause the outer case of the appliance to become live.

> **Objectives**
>
> In this section you will learn:
>
> the importance of a risk assessment
>
> the safety features of a mains circuit.

> **AQA Examiner's tip**
>
> When asked how the fuse works, do not use the phrase 'the fuse blows'. You should indicate that the fuse wire melts due to the heat generated by too much current flowing through it. The wire then breaks and isolates the live supply to the circuit.

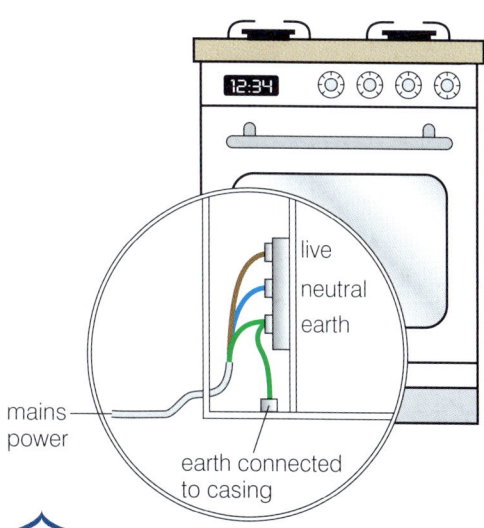

 A The earth lead connected to the metallic outer case of the cooker links back to the earth point when connected to the domestic mains ring

- Any appliance showing the symbol (Figure **B**) has an outer case which is doubly insulated and does not require an earth lead. Some desk lamps and hair dryers only require two-core mains cable since they have this type of insulation.
- The earth pin on a mains plug is the first pin to connect and the last to disconnect to provide maximum safety.
- The live and neutral terminals on the mains socket have safety shutters which are opened and closed by the earth pin on the plug.
- The switch on the power socket and on the appliance must be in the live lead so that the appliance can be isolated from the high energy supply.
- **Circuit breakers** are often installed at the main fuse box. Such devices are often thermal or magnetic and can be reset when the fault has been repaired.

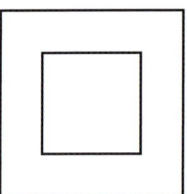

B *The symbol for double insulation*

Key terms

Risk assessment: taking into account possible dangers and modifying your actions so that you work safely.

PAT: Portable Appliance Testing.

Fuse: a common type of circuit breaker that contains a thin wire which melts to break the circuit when excess current flows.

Circuit breaker: usually an electromagnetic or thermal device that stops current flowing in a circuit because of a fault.

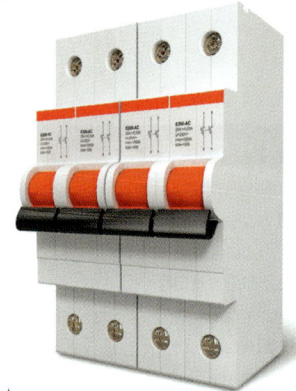

C *A magnetic circuit breaker*

A typical magnetic circuit breaker is shown in Figure **C**. (The particular type shown is an earth leakage circuit breaker or ELCB.) When in normal use, the iron rocker is attracted equally to both poles of the electromagnet. However, if a fault occurs and current runs to earth instead of through the neutral wire, the attraction from the neutral arm of the electromagnet is less strong and this tips the rocker so breaking the circuit.

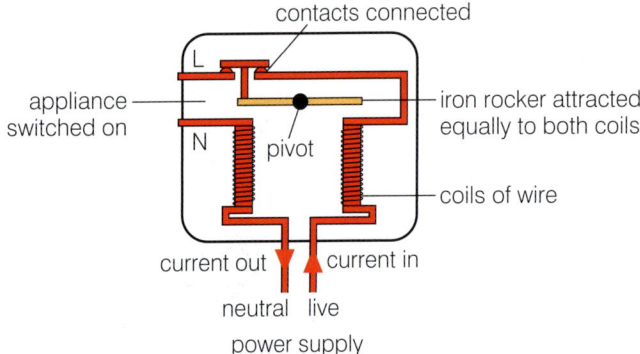

D *How a mains circuit breaker works*

Most types of circuit breaker make use of a magnetic or thermally controlled arm that trips a spring-loaded lever allowing the main contacts to spring open. This can then be reset once the fault in the circuit has been repaired. Although leakage to earth is the most common type of fault that circuit breakers detect, it should be remembered that they do not give complete protection against all possible faults.

Some of the issues that need to be considered when selecting the type of circuit breaker are:
- response time
- acceptable overload current
- the type of fault most likely to occur.

The selection of the most appropriate circuit breaker should be done in consultation with a qualified electrician.

Summary

Burns, sparks and explosions can be caused by both low voltage dc and high voltage ac mains circuits.

Mains electricity can cause an electric shock leading to muscle spasms, burns and fibrillation of the heart. This can be fatal.

Know your environment so that you can summon help and give basic first aid to a casualty suffering from an electric shock.

The three wires in a mains circuit are live, neutral and earth and should be correctly connected to a mains plug.

The prime safety features in a mains circuit are the fuse, earth wire, switch and circuit breaker.

A risk assessment involves knowing about the dangers and how to prevent them.

Questions

1. A qualified technician opens up a mains power supply to investigate a fault. Give one safety precaution he should take before:
   removing the case
   touching the components.

2. Why do the live and neutral pins on a mains plug have insulation covering the lower half of the pins?

3. Figure E shows the mains cable going into the metal case of a vacuum cleaner.
   a Explain why the vacuum cleaner should not be used.
   b Would you expect the wire to be two-core or three-core cable? Give a reason.
   c Why has a rubber grommet been used at the point where the cable enters the appliance?

4. Select the most appropriate fuse from (1 A, 2 A, 3 A, 5 A, 7 A, 10 A, 13 A) that should be used to protect a 1 kW electric fire plugged into a 230 V mains supply.

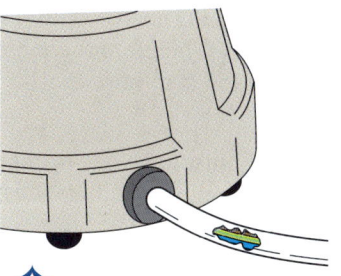

E *A vacuum cleaner and its mains cable*

2 Real electronic systems

2.1 What exactly is a system?

We use the term **system** to describe any collection of parts which together perform some useful function, or do a specific job. Figure **A** shows the insides of an electronic torch. Only a very few torches use filament bulbs these days. Most use an electronic light-producing component called a **light-emitting diode** or LED.

A *The insides of an LED torch*

The job of this system is to provide light. We call this the **output** of the system. In order for it to be able to do this it has to have things feeding into it. The power source – the 1.5 V battery – is one, and the signal from the switch is another. These are called **inputs**. They are, if you like, the 'raw materials' that the system needs so it can do its job.

Incidentally, the 1.5 V, AA, or AAA size battery that often powers electronic devices is not strictly a **battery** at all, but a **cell**. A battery is a number of cells wired together. For example, a 9 V battery is made up of six 1.5 V cells wired in series. However, you will rarely see them properly referred to as cells, so we will stick to battery.

The torch is a bit more complex than just a battery and a switch. The special white LED needs about 4 V to operate, but the battery only provides 1.5 V. Therefore there has to be an electronic unit (a circuit) whose function is to raise the 1.5 V to 4 V. This is an example of a **process**.

Any system must have one or more of each of these **input**, **process** and **output** sections, and we illustrate this with a **system diagram**, as shown in Figure **B**.

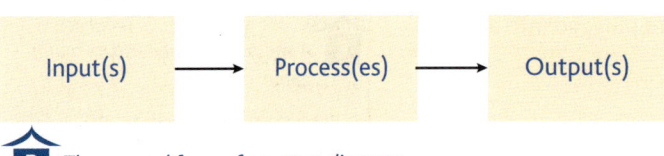

B *The general form of a system diagram*

The arrows linking the boxes indicate information flowing from one part of the system diagram to another – they are not connecting wires.

Objectives

In this section you will learn:

what an electronic system is

that a system consists of input, process and output sections

that the different 'blocks' within a system are called subsystems.

links

You will learn more about LEDs in Chapter 3.

Key terms

System: a collection of inputs, processes and outputs that together perform a task.

Light-emitting diode (LED): a component that only conducts in one direction and gives out light.

Output: the information coming out of a system that performs the required task.

Input: the information going into a system to provide it with its 'raw materials'.

Process: what is done to the inputs in order to create the outputs.

Chapter 2 Real electronic systems 15

2.2 Identifying the inputs and outputs of the system

The *actual* inputs and outputs of a system are almost always physical quantities, like heat, light, sound, or force. The electronic system itself can only process electrical signals (voltages or currents).

Transducers

One of the inputs to the torch comes from the switch, which is operated by someone pressing it. This means that the input to the system is really a force, and the switch converts this to a voltage, which can then be processed.

Devices like this that convert from one type of quantity to another are called **transducers**. If the state they convert to is an electrical signal, then they are at the input end of the system and are called **input transducers**. At the other end of the system, the LEDs are converting an electrical signal to light – which is the *actual* output of the system – so these are called **output transducers**.

System diagram of the LED torch

Since the whole point of electronic system diagrams is to help design and examine electronic systems, it is not usually any more helpful to show force etc. as system inputs and outputs. We know that a loudspeaker produces sound, for example, so there is little point in showing 'sound' as the system output. It is usual to simply show the transducers themselves as the inputs and outputs in a system diagram.

The system diagram for the LED torch looks like this:

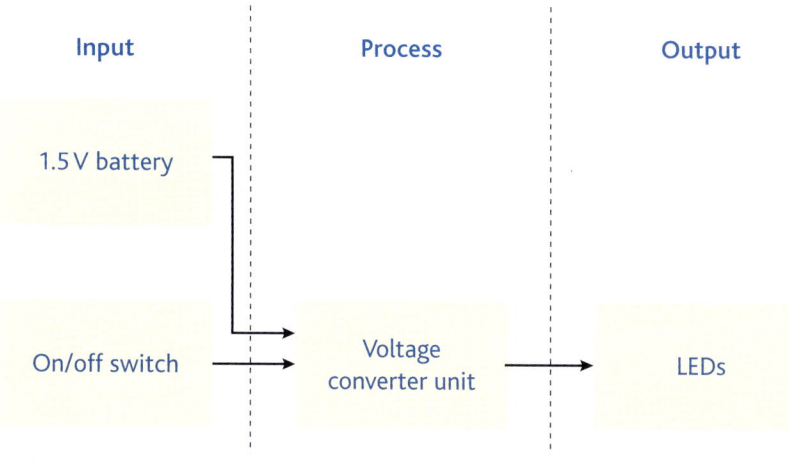

 The system diagram for the LED torch

We call each 'block' in the system a **subsystem**; so the LED torch system has four subsystems.

Objectives

In this section you will learn:

to appreciate that every system needs a power source

how to analyse a simple system and identify its subsystems

what a transducer is, and that most output transducers need a driver.

Key terms

Transducer: a device that converts from one type of quantity to another.

Input transducer: a transducer that converts a quantity into an electrical signal.

Output transducer: a transducer that converts an electrical signal into some other quantity.

Subsystem: an individual input, process or output within a system.

AQA Examiner's tip

Make sure you put subsystems in the right places. A process subsystem has information going in and coming out. An input subsystem only has information coming out of it. An output subsystem only has information going into it.

System diagram of a freezer alarm

Here is another example of a system. This one sounds an alarm when the temperature inside a freezer falls below a set limit.

Its system diagram is shown in Figure **B**. Notice that, as with most real systems, it has more than one subsystem in each section.

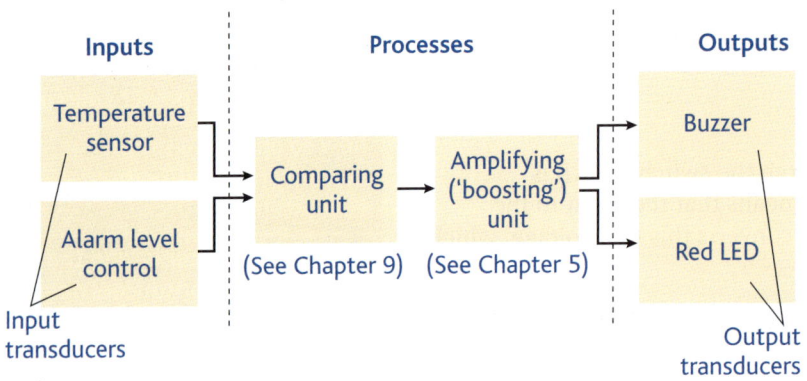

Key terms

Comparator: a circuit that compares two signals.

Transducer driver: a circuit that amplifies a signal so it can operate a transducer.

 B *The system diagram for a freezer alarm*

Inputs

The temperature sensor subsystem produces an electrical signal (a voltage) whose size depends on temperature (we say that the signal is the **analogue** of the temperature).

The alarm level control subsystem produces a fixed signal (voltage) according to the position the user sets it to. It would probably be a rotary dial, marked in °C. It sets the temperature at which the alarm will go off.

Processes

The comparing unit subsystem gives an output signal only when the temperature sensor signal exceeds the alarm level control signal.

Its output is only ever fully off or fully on (never in-between) so it is a **digital** signal. The proper technical name for a unit like this is a **comparator**.

The amplifying unit subsystem amplifies (or 'boosts') the output signal from the comparing unit subsystem so that it is powerful enough to drive the LED and the buzzer. It is needed because the electronic components usually used in the process subsystems do not have enough muscle to do this for themselves. The correct name for this type of subsystem is a **transducer driver**.

Outputs

The LED and buzzer subsystems convert the electrical signal from the amplifying unit into light and sound, respectively. So they both come on when the comparing unit subsystem is giving an output, which happens when the freezer temperature has risen above the set level.

The sort of freezer alarm that you can buy in the shops is usually a bit more complicated than this, because it has more features and provides

links

You will learn more about analogue signals in Chapter 9.

links

More information about digital signals can be found in Chapter 4 and about comparators in Chapter 9.

Chapter 2 Real electronic systems   17

more information for the user, although it is basically the same. The picture in Figure **C** shows a typical alarm, and its system diagram is shown in Figure **D**.

Most of the hard work is done in the processing subsystem labelled **Processor**. This is usually a small computer chip called a **microcontroller**.

> **Key terms**
>
> **Microcontroller**: computers on a single IC complete with memory and all the circuits needed for input and output.

links

You will learn more about microcontrollers in Chapter 13.

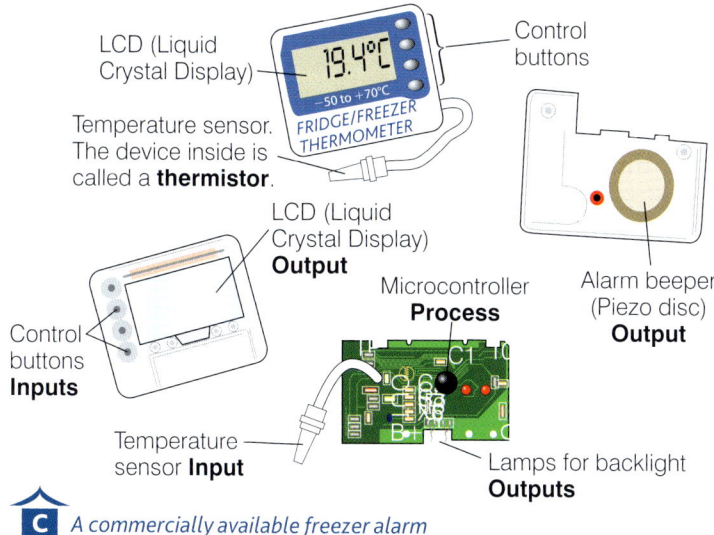

C A commercially available freezer alarm

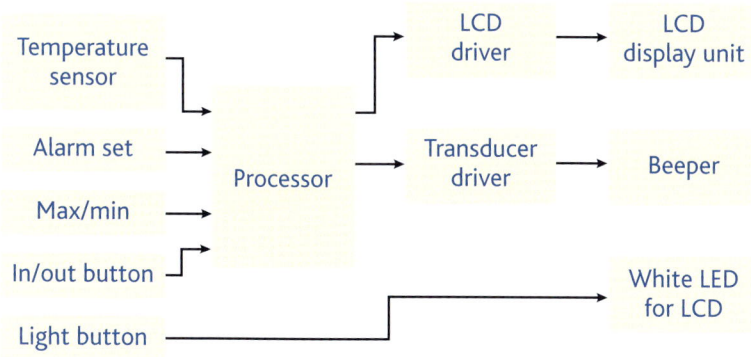

D A commercial freezer alarm system diagram

Notice that in neither of the two freezer alarm system diagrams have we shown the power source subsystem (i.e. the battery or cell). This is because every system must have one and it always does the same job. You should remember that it really ought to be there.

> **Activity**
>
> The best way to start finding out about electronic systems is to take an electronic gadget apart and have a look. (Make sure that it is your gadget, that you have removed or disconnected the batteries, and that you don't mind if it never works again!) Carefully take it apart. See if you can identify and list the inputs, processes and outputs. Draw a system diagram for the gadget, and write a simple explanation of what it does.

2.3 Designing systems

The real power of the system diagram becomes apparent when we use it to design an electronic system. This is because in modern electronics there are thousands of integrated circuits ('chips') and devices that can perform a huge range of different and often quite complicated functions – they are really whole systems in themselves. Once a system has been broken down into subsystems, and it is known what each of these has to do, chips or components that do each of these jobs can be put in. These can then be linked together to get a working system.

What follows shows you how to design a system. In this case, it's an intruder alarm, but whatever system you are designing, you should follow the same steps.

Designing an intruder alarm

1. Describe the function of the system.
2. Define the outputs of the system.
3. Define the inputs of the system.
4. Determine which processes are needed.
5. Draw the system diagram.

Describe the function of the system

The system must detect the movement of a person in the room and turn on a bright flashing light. It must also turn on a siren, but to avoid upsetting the neighbours the siren must turn off after 5 minutes. It must be possible to reset the system with a key-operated switch.

Define the outputs

There are just two – a flashing light and a siren. In a complex, commercial alarm system there might also be an output device that sends a coded signal or a pre-recorded message to the local police station via the telephone network, and even one which dials the owner's mobile to tell them there is a burglar in their house.

Define the inputs

As always we need a power source. Even though, as we said before, we don't need to show it on the diagram we must still decide what it is to be. Should it be a battery, or mains power? In practice, mains power would probably be the best choice since the alarm system would almost certainly be a permanent installation in the house. But for this exercise we'll stick with battery power – it's easier!

The most important input is a 'person sensor'. This will be a subsystem that provides a signal when it detects the movement of a person in the house.

The system will need an on-off switch, and a reset switch. These could be combined into one subsystem – a three-position switch marked 'ON–OFF-RESET'.

Determine which processes are needed

The person sensor signal will not be a constant one. It will come on when the person first enters the house, maybe go on and off as they move around, and then go off when they leave. In contrast, the alarm needs to

> **Objectives**
>
> In this section you will learn:
>
> to design a system from a given specification and draw its system diagram.

> **AQA Examiner's tip**
>
> When drawing a system, remember that a subsystem is a 'block' which does something, and so it has the name of the device or process which is doing it – it is not the description of an action. For example, *Motor* and *Counter* are both valid subsystems, but *Turn the Wheels* and *Count up to Ten* are not.

come on and then stay on. We need a subsystem that will turn on when it first receives a signal from the person sensor, and then keep it on. We'll call this a 'signal holding circuit'. Finally, for the siren we need a subsystem that will turn on when it receives a signal from the person sensor and automatically turn off after 5 minutes. We'll call this a 'timer circuit'.

Draw the system diagram

The last step is to put it all together and draw the system diagram.

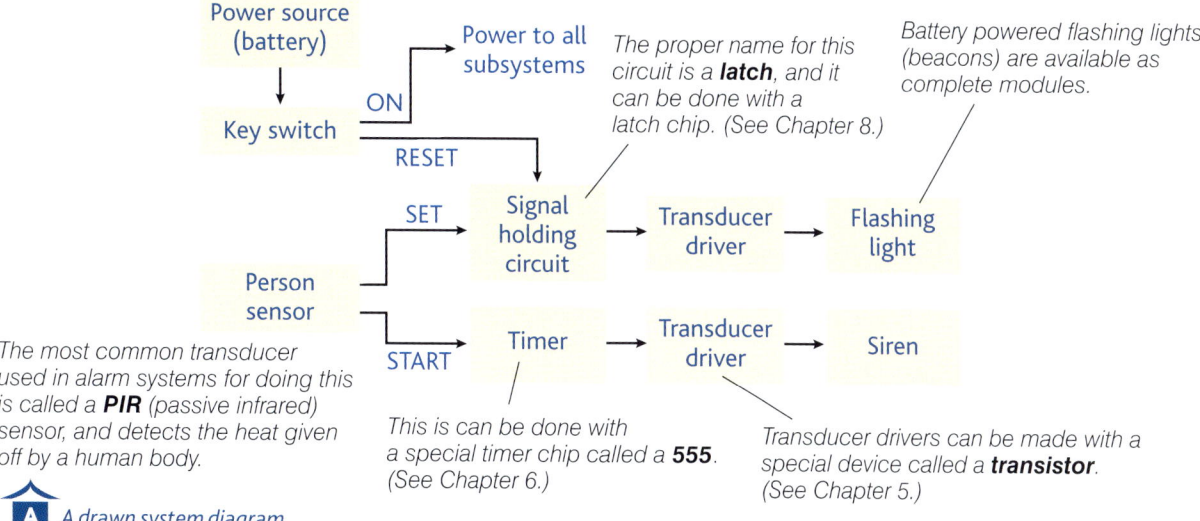

A A drawn system diagram

Summary

All electronic systems consist of one or more of each of these blocks: input, process and output.

The inputs, processes and outputs can be drawn as a system diagram, with links between the various parts indicating information flow.

The individual parts of a system are called subsystems.

Every electronic system needs a power source, even though this is usually omitted from the system diagram for clarity. Very often the power source is a battery.

Transducers are devices which convert one sort of quantity (e.g. sound, light, heat) into another. Input transducers convert an input quantity into an electrical signal, whilst output transducers convert an electrical signal into an output quantity.

Most electronic devices cannot produce enough power to drive things such as motors, lights, etc., and have to have their signals 'boosted'. This is done with a transducer driver.

To design a system, follow five basic steps:
1. Describe the function of the system.
2. State what outputs are wanted.
3. Decide what inputs will be required.
4. Work out what the processes have to be to convert the inputs to the outputs.
5. Draw the system diagram.

AQA Examiner's tip

It isn't always possible to put a system together like this, where each subsystem is a device or component straight off the shelf. Often, they have to be modified to make them do exactly what is wanted. Also, the output of one subsystem may have to be modified to suit the input of the next. This is called interfacing.

Questions

1 **a** Name the three basic sections that every system must have.
  b Pick an electronic system of your choice and see if you can describe accurately and clearly what the system does, making reference to the three basic sections.

2 Do some research to find out what the following transducers do, and then sort them into two lists – one list for input transducers, and one list for output transducers. In each case, state what the device is converting *from* and *to*.
microphone   LED   motor   solar cell   buzzer   electromagnet
reed switch   loudspeaker   radio aerial   thermistor

3 A friend asks you to design an electronic system to keep her goldfish pond topped up with water. She wants the water to be turned on when the level has dropped to a minimum point, and then turned off when it has filled up to the maximum level. You do some research and suggest the following subsystems which you think might be useful:

High water level switch	When immersed this subsystem gives out a signal. When uncovered it gives out no signal.
Low water level switch	When immersed this subsystem gives out no signal. When uncovered it gives out a signal.
Signal holding circuit	This subsystem has two inputs, called SET and RESET: When given a SET signal it turns its output on. When given a RESET signal it turns its output off.
Transducer driver	'Boosts' a signal so that it is powerful enough to drive an output transducer.
Motor controlled valve	This subsystem has two inputs, OPEN and CLOSE: When there is a signal at the OPEN input the valve opens, allowing water through and into the pond. When there is a signal at the CLOSE input the valve closes, shutting off the water.

Using as few or as many of the above subsystems as you need, draw a full system diagram and then describe how it works, referring to each of the subsystems in your description.

3 Building and testing a simple system

3.1 Basic equipment

Developing a circuit

All electronic circuits need a **dc power supply**, components and a means of holding the components together. There are a number of different prototyping boards on the market to aid construction. A prototyping board is simply a board on which a circuit can be developed. During the development stage, components may need to be replaced or repositioned and so any system that requires soldering can make this process more difficult. For this reason we will concentrate on using **breadboard** on which to construct our circuits.

It should be noted that breadboard does have its limitations, particularly in respect of high frequency, radio and high power work, but it should be more than adequate for the purposes of this course.

Breadboard

This is a plastic board with a series of holes arranged on a 0.1 inch (2.5 mm) grid into which jump leads, solid core connecting wire (22 gauge, 0.6 mm diameter) and the legs of components can be placed. At the bottom of each hole is a spring clip that forms a good electrical contact with the wire or component. Components and wires can be easily plugged in to the board to make the required connections and easily removed if changes need to be made.

> **Objectives**
> In this section you will learn:
> how a breadboard is used
> how to make and test a simple circuit.

> **Key terms**
> **dc power supply:** a power supply that produces direct current (a current that flows in one direction only).
> **Breadboard:** a solderless and reusable plastic base on which circuits can be quickly developed and tested.

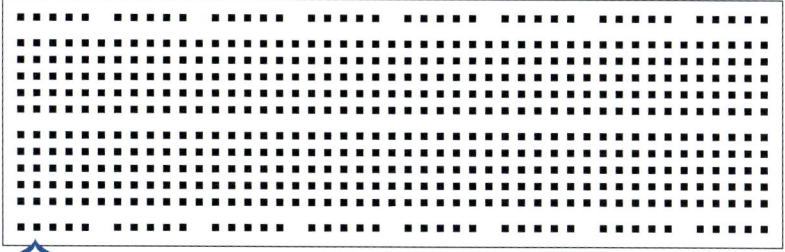

A A typical layout for a breadboard

It is important to know how the holes are connected inside the board in order to make use of it.

- **Horizontal connections:** The top and bottom rows (called bus bars) are both connected horizontally. Each set of five holes is connected to the next set as a continuous line. These are often used for the power supply lines. Some boards have double bus bars at the top and the bottom and can be used as independent rows.
- **Vertical connections:** Each set of five holes in a column are connected together. However, unlike the horizontal connectors, these connections stop at the end of each column of five holes.

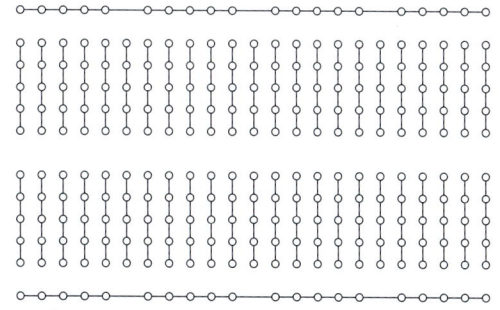

B The internal connections for a breadboard

In all activities we will assume the power supply to be 9 V, which can be taken from a PP3 battery or variable dc regulated power supply.

Activity

1 Checking the power lines on the breadboard

1. Place the (+) lead from your 9 V power supply in the top row of the breadboard and the (−) lead in the bottom row. These rows will now act as power rails.
2. Place a short jump lead so that it sticks up out of the far end of each rail (like a flag) to act as a test point. Use a voltmeter to check that the 9 V supply is getting across the board by putting a **digital multimeter (DMM)** set to a suitable dc voltage range, e.g. 20 V, across the flags. Never try to push the multimeter probes down the breadboard holes.

Key terms

Digital multimeter (DMM): a meter that allows you to switch to different modes to take voltage, current and resistance measurements using different ranges on the same meter.

Light-emitting diode (LED): a component that only conducts in one direction and gives out light.

Resistor: a component that controls the flow of current in a circuit.

Now that the board is ready for use, components and jump wires can be used to form a circuit enabling the electricity to flow from the top power rail to the bottom power rail.

Making a simple circuit

It would be useful to build a circuit indicator on the board to show when the power is on. A **light-emitting diode (LED)** can be used for this provided it is protected with a suitable **resistor**.

Being able to build circuits on breadboard by following a circuit diagram is an important skill. It does not matter if the breadboard does not have the same layout as that of the circuit diagram. What is important is that the route and sequence of components through which the current travels must be the same in both diagram and practical circuit.

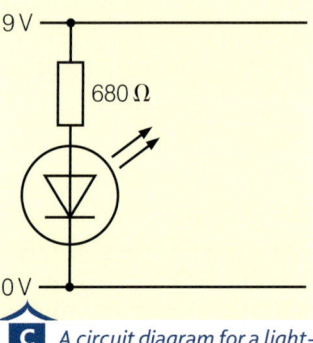

C A circuit diagram for a light-emitting diode indicator module

Activity

2 Building an LED indicator circuit

For this activity you will need a 9 V dc supply, a breadboard, a 680 Ω resistor (Figure **D**), a standard size red LED (Figure **E**), some wire links and a digital multimeter.

We need to set up the components as shown in Figure **F**, remembering to always pick up the electricity from the same column it was delivered to by the last component.

In order to put less stress on the legs of the LED, try using a jump wire to connect from the resistor in the upper half of the board to the lower half before picking up with the LED.

This circuit can now be used either to check the power on the breadboard or it can be adapted to act as an output indicator when testing other circuits. In the latter case, this circuit would be classified as an output subsystem.

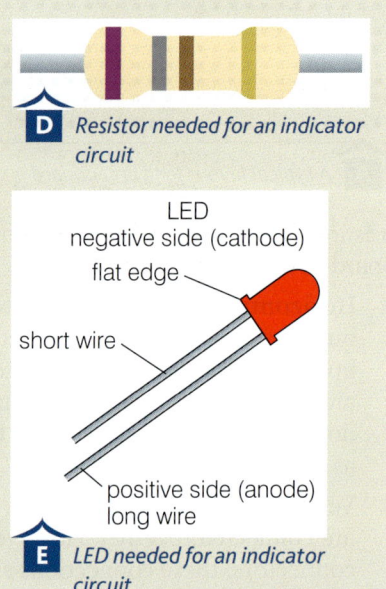

D Resistor needed for an indicator circuit

E LED needed for an indicator circuit

Chapter 3 Building and testing a simple system 23

Fault finding

Does the circuit work? If not we will need to find the fault. This is the start of a build and check regime which you should follow when you build any subsystem.

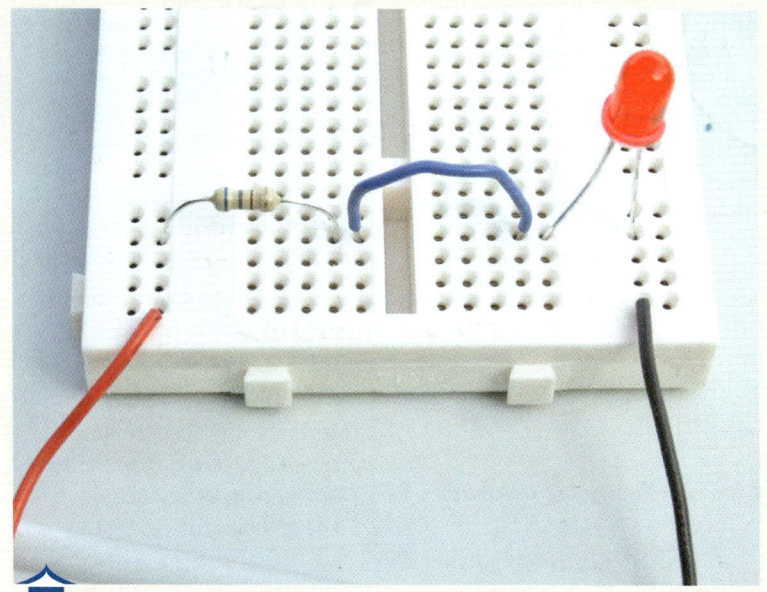

F *The completed breadboard circuit*

Checks to be made:

- Is the power from the supply the correct value? Check the value with a multimeter (0 mm) set to a suitable dc range, for example 20 V.
- Is the polarity of the power being supplied to the breadboard correct? The top rail should be (+) and the bottom rail (−). It is usual to make the (+) lead red and the (−) lead black.
- Is the voltage getting along the whole length of the breadboard? Use flags on the end of the breadboard and check with a voltmeter. It should give the same value as you had when you tested the power supply terminals.
- Is the resistor the correct value? If it is too large a value the LED will not light up, but if it is too small you may have destroyed the LED.
- Are all components and links following down the same column? Electricity cannot jump sideways from the columns without you making a route with a wire or component.
- Has the LED been placed facing the correct way round (polarity)?
- If the circuit still does not work, replace the LED with a new one.

3.2 Resistors

Before we can go much further, we need to look at resistors. Resistors can be found in most electronic circuits. Their main job is to control the flow of current through other components. However, in other chapters you will see them used as pull up/pull down resistors when used to generate digital signals from switches, etc. and as potential dividers when reference voltages are required. Resistors come in all different shapes and sizes and are made and used in a number of different ways. The more common types tend to be **carbon film,** or the better quality **metal film** fixed-value resistors. The unit for resistance is the **ohm (Ω)**.

> **Objectives**
>
> In this section you will learn:
>
> about the resistor as a basic component.

> **Key terms**
>
> **Ohm (Ω):** the unit of resistance.
>
> **Resistor colour code:** the system of coloured rings used on resistors to indicate their value in ohms.
>
> **Tolerance:** the acceptable error range due to the manufacturing and construction technique in the value of the resistor.

Fixed-value resistors

A A typical fixed value resistor with colour code shown as rings

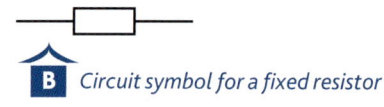

B Circuit symbol for a fixed resistor

Standard fixed-value resistors are easily recognisable by their shape and coloured bands. Fixed-value resistors are made typically in the range from $10\,\Omega$ to $10\,M\Omega$.

On a four-band resistor, the value can be obtained by using the **resistor colour code** to interpret the first three rings on the body of the resistor. The fourth ring may be separated slightly from the other bands and will usually be of a metallic colour. This ring indicates the **tolerance** (error) associated with the value.

The resistor colour code

The colours, corresponding numbers and the tolerance colours are shown in Tables **C** and **D**.

C

Number	Colour
0	black
1	brown
2	red
3	orange
4	yellow
5	green
6	blue
7	violet
8	grey
9	white

D

Tolerance	Colour
± 1%	brown
± 2%	red
± 5%	gold
± 10%	silver

To read the value of the resistor, position the tolerance band, usually silver or gold, on the right-hand side and then read the bands from left to right.

For the resistor shown in Figure **A**:

1st band – yellow;	2nd band – violet;	3rd band – red ;	4th band – gold
1st number	2nd number	Number of zeros	Tolerance/error
4	7	00	± 5%

This gives a value of 4700 Ω (4.7 kΩ).

So this resistor should have a value of 4700 Ω. The ± 5% is due to quality control limits in the manufacturing process and tells you the range in which the value should lie.

Its value will therefore be 4700 Ω ± 235 Ω. The resistor could have any value between 4465 Ω and 4935 Ω.

Activity

1 Resistor values

Take a number of resistors of the same value and check them with a DMM set to the resistance range. Always use a range which you think will accommodate the value and then place the DMM probes across the leads of the resistor. The DMM will provide the **voltage (potential difference or pd)** which will cause a current to flow for the test, so you should never have the power supply on when testing resistors in a circuit.

Do the values fall within the accepted range indicated by the colour code?

AQA Examiner's tip

Note how to use the colour code for low value resistors:
e.g. 22 Ω ±5%.
1st band – RED,
2nd band – RED
3rd band – BLACK
(no zeros are needed)
4th band – GOLD

Key terms

Voltage (potential difference or pd): the difference in energy levels in a circuit that causes the current to flow.

E24 series: a range of 24 numbers and their ×10 multipliers represent the values that resistors can have.

The E24 series

It is not possible to make every value of resistor that might be needed. The electronics industry, therefore, only produces resistors of particular values and these then form a series.

There are a number of different series available depending on how accurate you need the resistor to be and how much you want to pay. The **E24 series** provides an adequate range for most general purpose circuits.

The E24 series has 24 fixed numbers as shown in Table **E**.

E *The E24 series*

| 10 | 11 | 12 | 13 | 15 | 16 | 18 | 20 | 22 | 24 | 27 | 30 |
| 33 | 36 | 39 | 43 | 47 | 51 | 56 | 62 | 68 | 75 | 82 | 91 |

The numbers are chosen so that the ± 5% error range for each value gives an overlap with the next number in the series.

Resistors are made for each value in the series and also for a range of powers of 10.

For example, from the 22 value, you can obtain:
22 Ω, 220 Ω, 2200 Ω, 22 000 Ω, 220 000 Ω, 2 200 000 Ω.

AQA Examiner's tip

When choosing a resistor, always select the nearest value from the E24 series to the calculated value. However, if the selected value causes too much current to flow, you may have to choose the next highest value.

AQA Examiner's tip

When working out the colour code for a resistor, always write out the value in full before applying the code: e.g. 390 kΩ = 390 000 Ω.

The printed code (BS 1852)

Modern electronic components are gradually moving away from the colour code in favour of various printed codes. The BS 1852 **printed code** uses a mixture of numbers and letters as shown below.

The code is:

R means × 1   K means × 1000   M means × 1 000 000

The position of the letter gives the decimal point.

Tolerances are given by adding one of the following letters at the end of the code.

J means ± 5%,   K means ± 10%,   M means ± 20%

For example: 6K8J = 6.8 kΩ ± 5%
              39RK = 39 Ω ± 10%
              22KJ = 22 kΩ ± 5%

> **Key terms**
>
> **Printed code:** a means of using figures and letters to represent the value of a resistor.
>
> **Power rating:** the energy per second that the component is able to safely dissipate without suffering damage.

Resistor power rating

Not only can you obtain different value resistors from the preferred range, but each value will also be made with a range of **power ratings**.

When an electrical current passes through a resistor, heat is generated and the resistor must be able to withstand this so that it is not damaged or presents a Health and Safety issue to the user. Larger power resistors can be recognised by their larger physical size as shown in Figure **F**.

Common power rating values are:

$\frac{1}{8}$ W, $\frac{1}{4}$ W, $\frac{1}{2}$ W, 1 W, 2 W, 5 W

When selecting a resistor, the power rating should always exceed the value that has been calculated as being the power output from the resistor. This is usually the next nearest value above that calculated.

In modern electronic circuits, the currents are so low that the $\frac{1}{8}$ W range can usually be used.

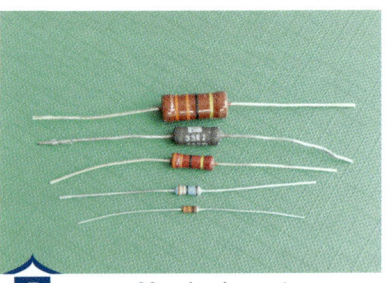

F *Series of fixed-value resistors showing different power ratings*

> **Activity**
>
> **2 Fixed resistors**
>
> Do some research to find out more about the following types of fixed resistor:
> - The DIL resistor chip
> - The wire-wound resistor
> - The surface-mounted resistor.
>
> Concentrate on:
> What is special about the resistor?
> Where might the resistor be used?

3.3 Light-emitting diodes (LEDs)

All LEDs are part of the diode family (components that will only allow current to flow in one direction). However, the LED has the extra property of giving out light when current flows through it and as such it is often used as an indicator. Figure **A** shows both the component and the circuit symbol used.

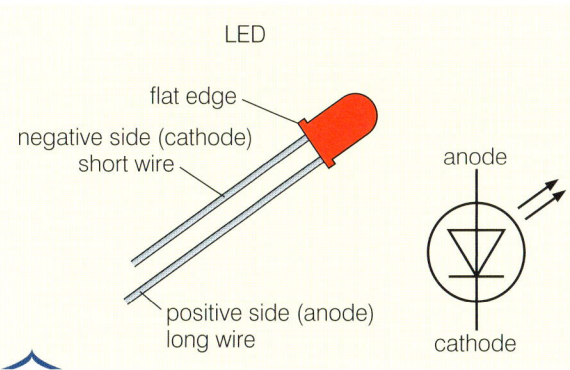

A *An LED and its circuit symbol*

Objectives
In this section you will learn:
- more about the light-emitting diode (LED).

Key terms
Forward bias: applying the voltage across a diode in such a way so that the diode is able to conduct.

Reverse bias: applying a voltage across a diode in such a way that it will block the flow of current.

■ Technical information (general)

- On the real component, the short leg or the leg next to the flat section of the package rim is the cathode (−).
- When a voltage is applied to make the LED conduct, the component is said to be **forward biased**, but if applied so that there is no conduction then it is **reverse biased**.

■ Technical information (numerical)

Numerical information is normally found in any good catalogue selling the components and may vary depending on the type of LED you use. Below are some typical data for a standard 5mm red LED. Obtaining and understanding the technical information from various sources will be part of your developing research skills.

- V_F is the voltage drop across the LED when used in forward bias mode.
- I_{Ftyp} is the typical current that might be allowed to flow through the LED.
- I_{Fmax} is the maximum current that should be allowed to flow through the LED.
- For a standard 5 mm red LED, typical values might be:
  $V_F = 2\,V$; $I_{Ftyp} = 10\,mA$; $I_{Fmax} = 30\,mA$.

We know that an LED offers little resistance to the current once it starts to conduct. We therefore need to use a resistor to control the current flow.

The calculation for the protective resistor goes as follows:

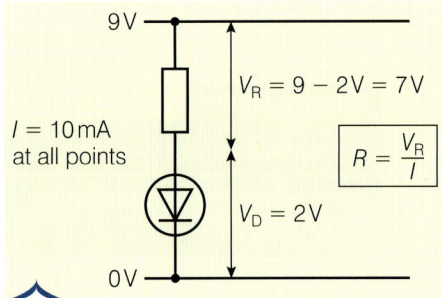

B Calculation for the protective resistor in a diode circuit

- If a 9 V supply is used and the LED uses 2 V to make itself conduct, that leaves 9 V − 2 V = 7 V. This is the excess voltage in the circuit.
- The excess must be used up across a resistor placed in series with the LED. (The total voltages in a series circuit must add up to the supply voltage.)
- The resistor must carry the same **current** as the LED. (Currents in a series circuit are the same at all points.)
- Now the value of R can be calculated using **Ohm's law**.
- Local values (those that relate to the resistor only) are used.
- Let V_R be the voltage across the resistor.
- Let I_R be the current through the resistor.

$$R = \frac{V_R}{I_R}$$

$$R = \frac{7\,V}{10\,mA}$$

$$R = 700\,\Omega$$

The nearest E24 value is 680 Ω.

If it is important that the current does not exceed 10 mA, then the next highest value should be used (i.e. 750 Ω).

Key terms

Current: the quantity of electrical charge flowing per second through a point in a circuit.

Ohm's law: the current through a resistor at constant temperature is directly proportional to the potential difference across the resistor: $\left(I = \frac{V}{R}\right)$

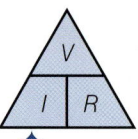

C Formula triangle for Ohm's law

Hint

The equation for Ohm's law can be written in three different ways:

$$V = IR$$
$$R = \frac{V}{I}$$
$$I = \frac{V}{R}$$

They are all the same equation, just rearranged. See the formula triangle, Figure **C**.

Summary

Breadboard and circuit diagrams both use the idea of power rails.

When constructing even the simplest of circuits, adopt a build-and-test approach together with a logical/sequential approach to fault finding.

Resistors are used to control the flow of current through a component.

Resistors can be identified using the colour code and the BS 1852 printed code.

The E24 series is a range of 24 resistor values which together with their powers of 10 are appropriate for general use.

The power of a resistor is its ability to cope with the heat generated and this will determine its construction and physical size. The power rating must always be larger than the power that the resistor will dissipate in the circuit.

An LED only allows current to flow in one direction and can be used as a circuit indicator. It must be protected with a resistor in series with it.

Chapter 3 Building and testing a simple system

Questions

1 A student builds the LED indicator circuit on breadboard following the instructions in Activity 1. The student checks the power supply terminals with a voltmeter and confirms that there is 9 V on the terminals. They notice that the LED fails to light up. State and explain four possible faults the circuit could have.

2 Answer this question using the resistor colour code.
  a What value resistor has the colour code Brown Black Orange Gold?
  b What range of values could this resistor have?

3 What value resistor has the colour code:
  a RED   PURPLE   YELLOW   GOLD
  b ORANGE   WHITE   RED   SILVER
  c BROWN   GREY   BLACK   GOLD

4 A resistor is calculated to have a value of 2500 Ω.
  a Which E24 series resistor should be selected?
  b Which E24 series resistor should be used if the 2500 Ω is the calculated value based on the maximum current allowed through the component it is protecting?

5 What value resistor has the printed code:
  a 2K7K
  b 82RJ
  c 2M2J

6 The calculated power from a resistor is 0.3 W. Which power rating resistor should be used?
Select from the following. $\frac{1}{8}$ W, $\frac{1}{4}$ W, $\frac{1}{2}$ W, 1 W, 2 W, 5 W.

7 The student looks up details for an LED to find the following:
$V_F = 1.8$ V
$I_{Ftyp} = 20$ mA
  a What current will be expected to flow through the protective resistor?
  b What voltage will there be across the protective resistor if the circuit is run on 15 V?
  c Find the value of the protective resistor that should be used for the LED when used with this power supply.
  d What value resistor should be selected from the E24 series if a current of 20 mA is not to be exceeded?
  e What power rating should the E24 resistor, selected in part **d**, have if it has to cope with up to 20 mA flowing through it?

4 Decision making circuits

4.1 Switches

Digital electronic circuits are found in computers, telephones, MP3 players and almost every electronic device. They all use the same basic principle, which is simple because it uses only two states, 0 and 1. Digital electronic circuits are sometimes called logic circuits because they use **logic gates** which work according to simple, logical rules. Digital circuits use voltages to represent the 0 and 1.

So, in digital electronics there are only two voltages allowed: a **high voltage** and a **low voltage**. The opposite of digital is **analogue** where you can have any voltage between the minimum and maximum.

What are switches?

Switches are used as inputs in digital electronics. When a switch is **closed** it is on; it conducts electricity. When a switch is **open** it is off; it does not conduct electricity.

When a switch is used as an input to a digital circuit, it is **always** used in series with a resistor. The switch and resistor are **always** connected between the power supply connections. The logic signal from the switch is **always** taken from where the switch connects to the resistor.

> **Objectives**
>
> In this section you will learn:
>
> how to select and describe the use of switches
>
> about the use and application of a pull-up/pull-down resistor
>
> that a digital system uses a voltage signal that is either at a high level or low level and that these states are represented by 1 or 0, respectively.

> **Key terms**
>
> **Digital:** a signal that can only have two values, high or low.
>
> **Logic gates:** a component that combines digital signals.
>
> **High voltage:** represents 1.
>
> **Low voltage:** (usually 0 V) represents 0.
>
> **Switch:** a device used to connect and disconnect a circuit.

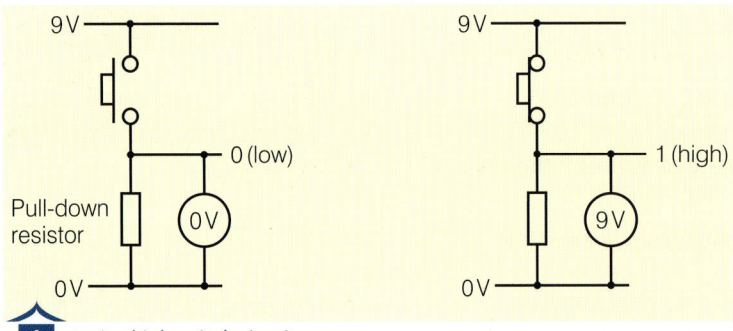

A *Active high switch circuits*

In Figure **A**, when the switch is closed, the output from the switch is 1 (high) because the switch connects the output to the supply voltage. When the switch is open, the output is 0 (low) because it is connected to 0 V through the resistor. The resistor is sometimes called a 'pull-down resistor' because it pulls the output down to 0 V. The pull-down resistor usually has a value in kΩ. The exact value does not matter as long as we put one there.

Digital switch inputs that work the other way around can be used so that the signal is 0 when the switch is pressed.

Chapter 4 Decision making circuits

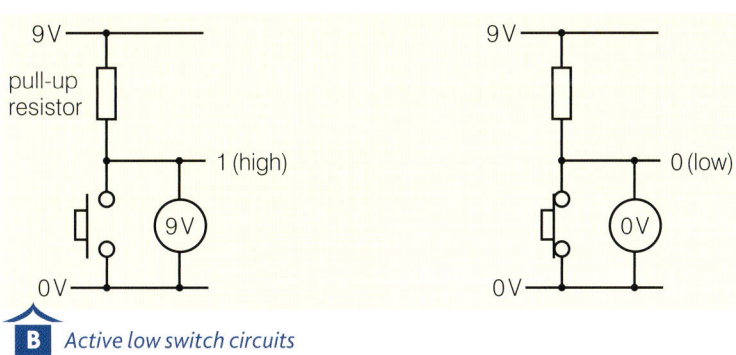

B Active low switch circuits

> **AQA Examiner's tip**
> Look out for floating inputs!

In Figure **B**, when the switch is closed, the output from the switch is 0 (low) because the switch connects the output to 0 V. When the switch is open, the output is 1 (high) because it is connected to the supply voltage through the resistor. The resistor is sometimes called a 'pull-up resistor' because it pulls the output up to the supply voltage.

If we left the resistor out of the switch circuit then the circuit would not be reliable. When the switch was not pressed we would not know what the voltage at the output was, and the logic level will depend on any interference picked up by the circuit – we call this a **floating** output. Floating signals cause random behaviour in digital circuits so we need to avoid them by using pull-down or pull-up resistors.

Types of switches

There are lots of different types of switches:

- A simple push switch (Figure **C**) is closed only while the button is pressed, e.g. a doorbell switch.
- A toggle switch (Figure **D**) can be moved to stay in the open or closed position, e.g. a light switch.
- A microswitch (Figure **E**) is like a push switch but is usually operated by a machine, e.g. the switch which senses if the door on a microwave is open.
- A reed switch (Figure **F**) is closed when a magnet is near it, e.g. a switch that senses if a door is open.
- A tilt switch (Figure **G**) is closed or open depending on whether it is vertical or horizontal, e.g. a switch in a vending machine that senses if it is being tilted.

C Push switches

D Toggle switches

E Microswitches

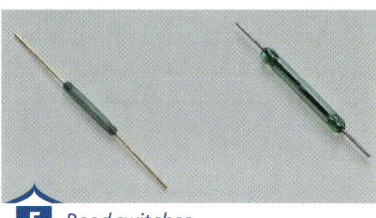

F Reed switches

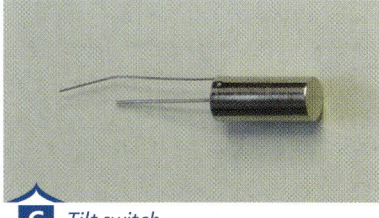

G Tilt switch

4.2 Logic gates

Logic gate rules and truth tables

Sometimes more than one input is needed in a circuit. When you want to combine two or more digital signals you use logic gates. Logic gates obey simple rules.

This behaviour can be shown in table called a **truth table**. A truth table shows all the possible inputs (00, 01, 10 and 11) and shows the output in each case.

The output of an **AND** gate is 1 only when both of the inputs are 1.

The AND gate

input A	input B	output C
0	0	0
0	1	0
1	0	0
1	1	1

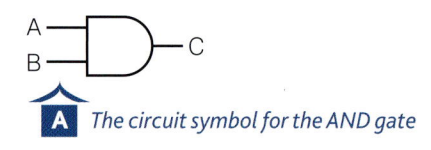

A The circuit symbol for the AND gate

The NOT gate

The NOT gate is a special kind of gate with only one input. The output of a NOT gate is the opposite of its input. The truth table for a NOT gate is simple because there are only two lines.

input D	output E
0	1
1	0

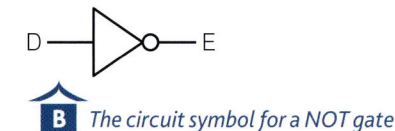

B The circuit symbol for a NOT gate

The OR gate

The OR gate has a high output when input F is high OR input G is high OR both are high. Notice that the OR gate symbol has a pointed front and curved back and sides.

input F	input G	output H
0	0	0
0	1	1
1	0	1
1	1	1

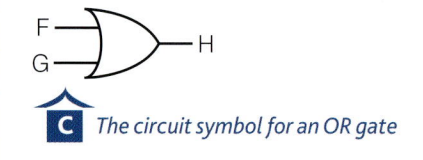

C The circuit symbol for an OR gate

Objectives

In this section you will learn:

to explain that a logic gate is a device with one output and several inputs and the output is either at a high level or a low level depending on the inputs

to draw the symbols and truth tables for the logic gates AND, NAND, OR, NOR and NOT and write down their behaviour

to use truth tables to determine the output of a combination of logic gates

to solve system problems, stated in words, using combinations of logic gates

to draw a layout of a circuit and assemble a circuit following a circuit diagram.

Key terms

Truth table: a table that shows all of the possible inputs and outputs of a logic circuit.

Chapter 4 Decision making circuits

The NAND gate

The NAND gate is easy to remember because NAND means NOT AND so the truth table is the opposite of the AND gate truth table. The symbol for a NAND gate is an AND gate symbol with a circle on the end – the circle means NOT.

input J	input K	output L
0	0	1
0	1	1
1	0	1
1	1	0

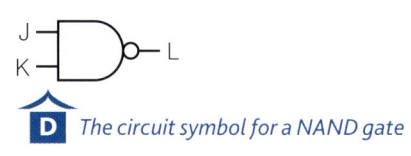

D The circuit symbol for a NAND gate

> **AQA Examiner's tip**
> Make sure you have learnt the symbols and truth tables for each of the five logic gates: AND, NAND, OR, NOR and NOT. Try closing your book and drawing the symbol and truth table for each logic gate from memory.

The NOR gate

NOR means NOT OR so the truth table for the NOR gate is the opposite of the OR gate truth table. The symbol for a NOR gate is an OR gate symbol with a circle on the end – again, the circle means NOT.

input M	input N	output Q
0	0	1
0	1	0
1	0	0
1	1	0

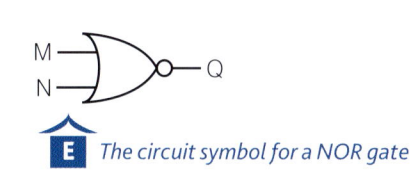

E The circuit symbol for a NOR gate

Testing logic gates

We can test that an AND gate works as we expect by building a circuit with an AND gate in it and trying it out.

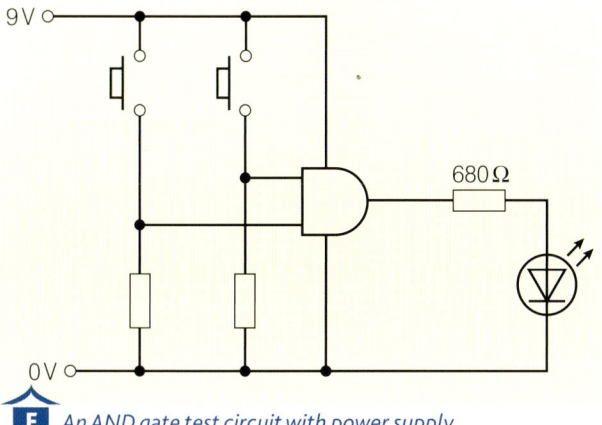

F An AND gate test circuit with power supply

Normally, to make the diagram simpler, we do not draw the power supply to the logic gates in the circuit diagram.

Key terms

ICs: integrated circuits.

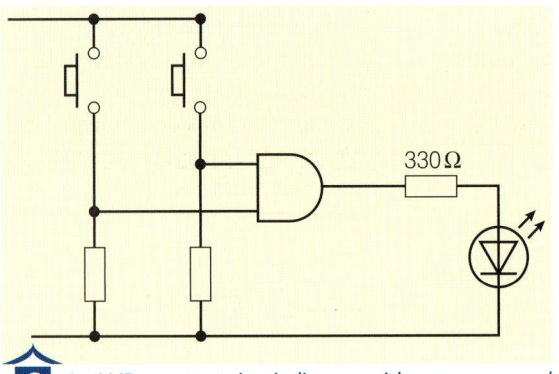

G An AND gate test circuit diagram without power supply

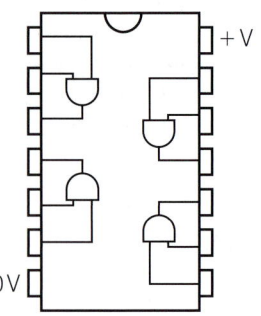

H A 4081 AND gate IC and its pinout

The switches are the two inputs to the AND gate. The LED is the output. When a switch is pressed it makes that input 1 (high, 5 V). When the output of the logic gate is 1 the LED will glow.

Logic gates come in **ICs** that have four or six logic gates in them. Whichever logic gate you use you must remember to connect the power supply pins.

Pins on ICs

ICs are complete electronic circuits in a single package. Having a complete circuit in a small package makes things small, cheap and fast, and makes microelectronics possible. The IC was such a good idea that one of the inventors, Jack Kilby, was awarded a Nobel Prize in 2000 for his work which originated in 1958. Unfortunately the other inventor, Robert Noyce, died before the prize was given.

ICs are usually black pieces of plastic with pins down two sides and letters and numbers on the top which tell you what type it is. To get the IC the correct way around there is a small piece cut out or a small dot on the left-hand side. The pins are given numbers starting with 1 underneath the cut out or dot and then counting along the bottom from left to right. When you get to the end continue counting from right to left along the top, Figure **I**.

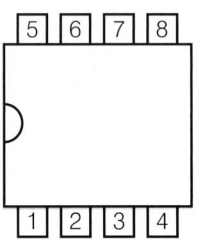

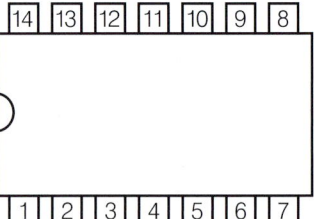

I 8-pin and 14-pin ICs with pins numbered

Activity

Have a go at building a circuit to test the AND gate. Draw and fill in a truth table for the AND gate using your circuit.

Change your circuit to check the truth tables for an OR gate, a NOR gate and a NAND gate.

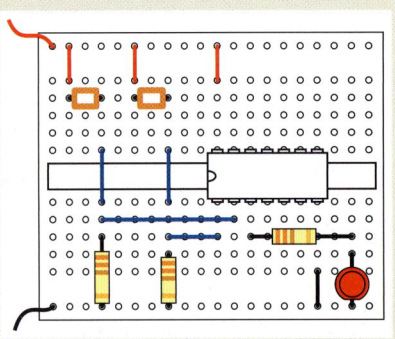

AQA Examiner's tip

Some circuits may be unreliable if the inputs to unused gates are left floating.

Combining logic gates

To solve real problems, several logic gates need to be connected together. You can work out how the circuit will behave by drawing a truth table for the whole circuit. The truth table will show the output of the circuit for every possible combination of inputs. There are two possible values for an input, so if the circuit has two inputs, the truth table will have 2 × 2 = 4 lines. If the circuit has three inputs, the truth table will have 2 × 2 × 2 = 8 lines.

To make it easier to draw the truth table, label the output of every gate in the circuit with a different letter and add a column in the truth table for every letter.

An example

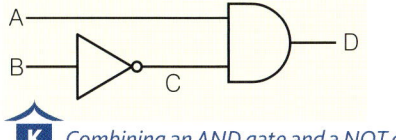

K *Combining an AND gate and a NOT gate*

Draw the truth table with four lines because there are two inputs. Fill in the inputs A and B with all the possible combinations.

A	B	C	D
0	0		
0	1		
1	0		
1	1		

C = NOT B so write C as the opposite of B.

A	B	C	D
0	0	1	
0	1	0	
1	0	1	
1	1	0	

D = C AND A so D is only 1 when C and A are both high.

A	B	C	D
0	0	1	0
0	1	0	0
1	0	1	1
1	1	0	0

This shows that D is only high when A is high and B is low.

When the inputs and outputs of the logic gates are shown on the diagram you can find out how the circuit works by writing on the truth table, Figure **L**.

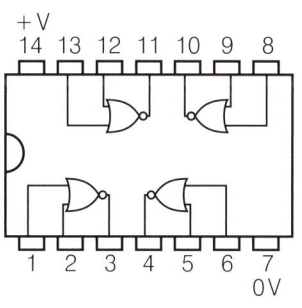

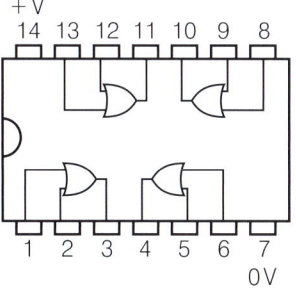

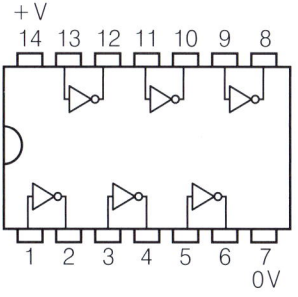

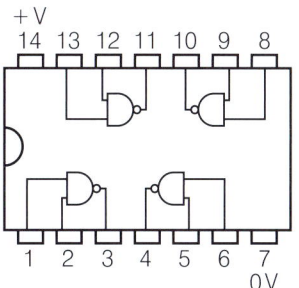

J *Pinouts of logic gates*

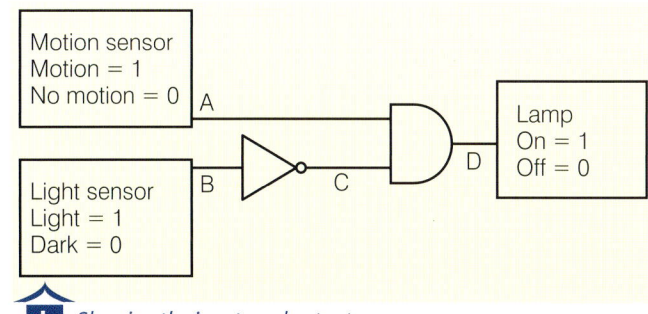

L *Showing the inputs and outputs*

To find out how the circuit works, copy down the truth table and write in the inputs and outputs. You can then read how the circuit works from the truth table.

A	B	C	D
0 No motion	0 Dark	1	0 Lamp off
0 No motion	1 Light	0	0 Lamp off
1 Motion	0 Dark	1	1 Lamp on
1 Motion	1 Light	0	0 Lamp off

This shows that the lamp is only on when the motion is sensed and it is dark.

Designing logic circuits

When you want to design a logic circuit to solve a problem, you need to have a clear description of what it needs to do. Think about where to use the words 'and', 'or' and 'not' in your description. First you need to identify the inputs and outputs of your system. To see how the truth table relates to what you are trying to build, it sometimes helps to write it down first.

For example, the doors in a car unlock when the key is turned in the lock or the remote control code is received. The key switch produces a high when the key is turned. The remote control gives a 1 when the correct code is sensed. The car lock is unlocked with a 0 and locked with a 1.

You can see that the inputs are the key switch and the remote control sensor and the output is the lock.

The truth table will have four lines because there are two inputs, so all four of the possible inputs are filled in.

Now fill in the lock column with 'unlocked' and 'locked' on the correct lines and put the 0s and 1s with the correct descriptions.

key switch	remote control sensor	lock
0 (no key)	0 (no code received)	locked 1
0 (no key)	1 (correct code received)	unlocked 0
1 (key turned)	0 (no code received)	unlocked 0
1 (key turned)	1 (correct code received)	unlocked 0

This is the truth table for a NOR gate so the solution is as shown below.

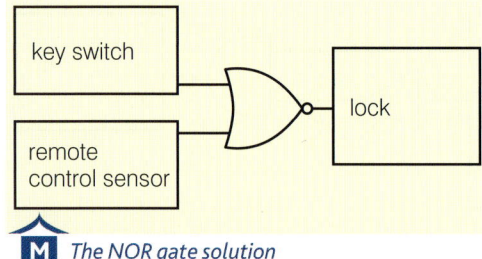

M *The NOR gate solution*

Chapter 4 Decision making circuits

Summary

Switches can be used as inputs in digital electronics.

Switches in digital electronics are always connected in series with a resistor.

When a pull-down resistor is used, the output is 1 when the switch is closed. When a pull-up resistor is used, the output is 0 when the switch is closed.

A logic gate is a component that combines digital signals.

The five logic gates you need to know about are AND, OR, NOT, NAND, NOR.

Truth tables tell you what a logic circuit does.

In a complex logic circuit the truth table should have a column for each input and for every gate output.

Logic circuits can be designed by drawing the truth table for the system and then seeing which logic gates will produce the same truth table.

Questions

1. Find some examples of situations in which each of the types of switch in Topic 4.1 are used.

2. Use a diagram to show how to use a reed switch to produce a logic 1 signal when a magnet is near the reed switch. How would you change the circuit to produce a logic 0 signal when a magnet is near the reed switch?

3. Draw and complete the truth table for the circuits in Figure **N** and Figure **O**.

4. Draw a 20-pin IC with all of the pins correctly numbered.

5. Draw a picture of how to connect a NOT gate to a switch and LED on a prototype board to test its truth table.

6. Design a circuit that will turn on a warning light when someone sits in a car and does not put on their seat belt. The pressure sensor in the seat gives a logic 1 when someone sits in the seat and the seatbelt catch produces a logic 1 when the seatbelt is on. The warning light comes on with a logic 1.

7. Design a system that will turn on a heater when it gets cold during the day. The temperature sensor produces a 0 when it is cold and the light sensor produces a 1 in the dark. A logic 1 is needed to turn the heater on.

8. Close your book and draw the symbol, name and truth table for all five logic gates.

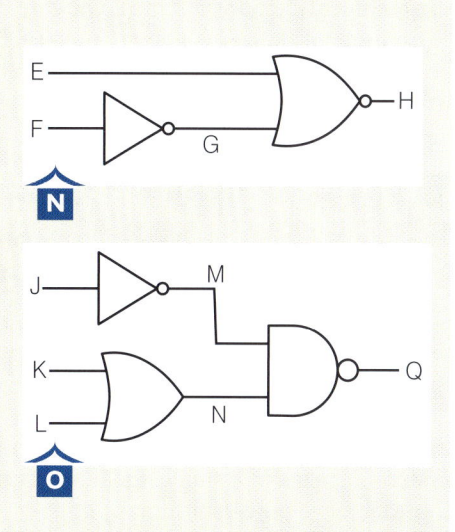

5 Boosting the signal

5.1 Transducer drivers using transistors

In Chapter 2, when we looked at systems, we said that in nearly all cases the signals are too weak to drive things like buzzers, motors etc. Figure **A** shows an idea for an electronic system that can be used to illustrate the problem.

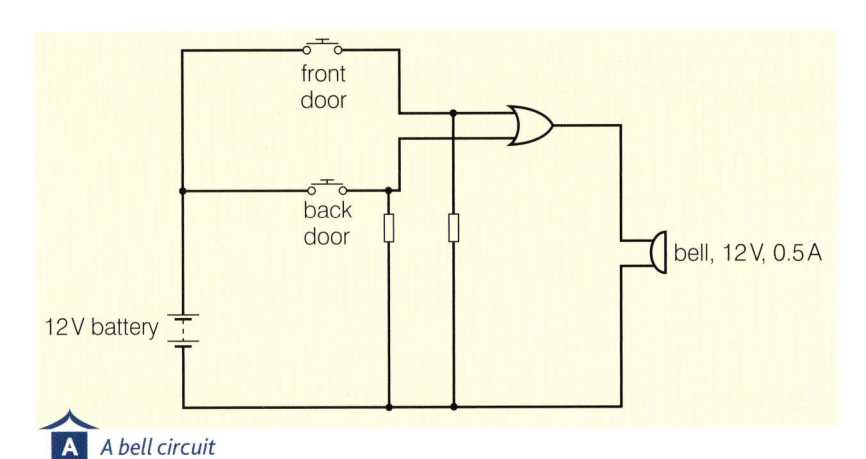

A *A bell circuit*

> **Objectives**
>
> In this section you will learn:
>
> when and why a transducer driver is needed in a system
>
> the symbols and lead names for the BJT and the MOSFET
>
> how to use the BJT and the MOSFET as transducer drivers
>
> what a protection diode is and know how it is connected
>
> to appreciate the differences between the BJT and the MOSFET.

This system is designed to sound the electric bell if either the front doorbell switch *or* the back doorbell switch is pressed. If you look up the technical data for a typical OR gate, it says that the maximum current it can deliver is about 2 mA (0.002 A). However, the particular bell for this system needs 0.5 A to operate. The OR gate would not work.

links
You have already met transducers in Chapter 2.

What is a transducer driver?

The signals need to be 'boosted' or amplified first. This is done using a **transducer driver**. As is usual in electronics there are many ways in which this can be done; we are going to look at the two most important ones.

In about 1946, three enterprising eggheads in America invented the **transistor**. This device is just what we need for our doorbell system. It takes in a small signal and turns it into a more powerful signal.
There are two types of transistor - the **bipolar junction transistor** (or **BJT**) and the **MOSFET**, and transducer drivers that use them are often called **transistor switches**. Physically, the two types look similar, and they come in a wide variety of cases (or **packages**) and sizes, Figure **B**.

B *Common transistors*

Chapter 5 Boosting the signal

■ The bipolar junction transistor (or BJT)

Figure **C** shows the electronic circuit symbol for the BJT, and the names of the three connecting wires.

How does it work? The BJT is made from a semiconductor material (usually silicon), and three different types of it are sandwiched together. The process by which it amplifies is quite complicated, but you do not need to know the details. Here is a simplified explanation:

You can think of the BJT as an electronically controlled water valve, where a small signal controls the opening of the valve and thus the water flow between the water supply tank and the output pipe. This is shown in Figure **D**.

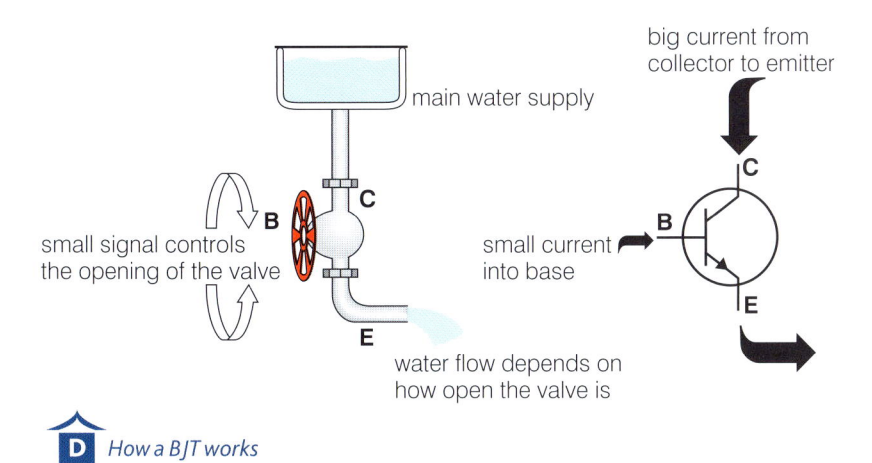

C *The BJT*

D *How a BJT works*

The main water supply is equivalent to the power supply for the electronic system. The signal controlling the valve is the current flowing into the **base**, i.e. the signal we want to boost, and the high water flow down through the valve is the boosted current flowing from **collector** to **emitter** in the transistor – the one we want to use in our output transducer. The larger the input (base) current, the greater is the output (collector) current (within limits!).

The amount by which the current is amplified is called the **current gain**, and the size of this depends on the particular BJT you use – you can get ones that have gains between about 25 and 500. Figure **E** shows how the BJT is actually connected to make a transducer driver – in this case, one for boosting the signal from the OR gate to drive our doorbell.

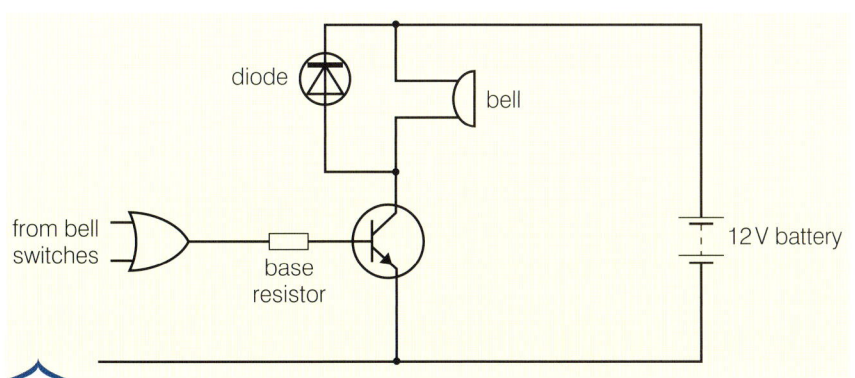

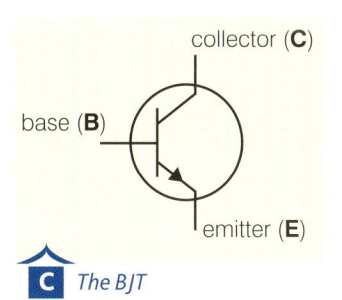

E *The BJT connected as a transducer driver*

Key terms

Transducer driver: a circuit that 'boosts' or amplifies a signal so that it can operate a transducer.

Transistor: a component that boosts a signal.

BJT: stands for Bipolar Junction Transistor.

MOSFET: stands for Metal Oxide Semiconductor Field Effect Transistor.

Base, collector, emitter: the three terminals of a BJT.

Current gain: the amount by which the signal is amplified.

AQA Examiner's tip

There are two types of BJT: The NPN type, shown here, and the PNP type. You only need to know the NPN type.

The **base resistor** is needed because the BJT is quite a delicate device, and if the base current were too large it could damage or destroy it. For this reason it is often called a **current limiting** resistor.

The diode across the motor is very important. It is used as a **protection diode** – to protect the BJT against the large voltage surge that is generated when it turns off. This only happens when it is driving electromagnetic devices – such as motors and solenoids (an electric bell works by using an electromagnet – a solenoid). It is not needed for other output devices.

> **Key terms**
>
> **Base resistor:** the resistor that connects between the signal to be amplified and the base of the BJT.
>
> **Protection diode:** a diode connected across the transducer to protect the transistor from being damaged by the high voltage surge when the transistor switches off.
>
> **Gate, Source, Drain:** the three terminals of a MOSFET.

Activity

One of the best ways to show just how good the BJT is for amplifying signals is to use two of them, and connect the output of one into the input of the second one. This produces a huge amplification – so large that it can produce enough current to drive a motor just from a tiny current through your finger. The circuit in Figure **F** shows how.

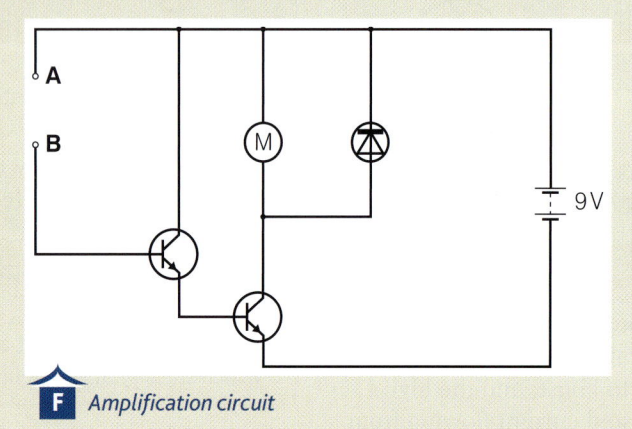

F Amplification circuit

Any BJTs will do, provided they have a current gain of 100 or more.

Touching your finger across the two wires A and B – even very lightly – should make the motor turn. Prove that the transducer driver is necessary: try to get the motor to run by connecting the battery directly to the motor via your finger!

> **AQA Examiner's tip**
>
> Make sure you draw the diode round the right way in the circuit diagram! If it is the other way up it means that the current will bypass the bell (or motor, or whatever it is the transistor is switching) altogether. Remember that current always flows through a diode from the anode (the triangle) to the cathode (the line).

The MOSFET

The full name for this device is **metal oxide semiconductor field effect transistor**. The MOSFET is also an ideal candidate for our doorbell system, but it works in a very different way to the BJT. Figure **G** shows the electronic circuit symbol of the MOSFET, and the names of the three connecting wires.

How does it work? Thinking of the MOSFET as an electronically controlled water valve is still a good way to understand the process, but instead of the valve being controlled by a current it is controlled by a voltage. No current at all is needed by the gate of the MOSFET. The bigger the voltage on the **gate**, the more the valve is opened and thus the greater the output flow between the **drain** and the **source**. The

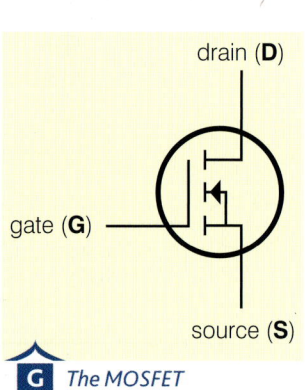

G The MOSFET

MOSFET can tolerate big voltages on its gate (within reason), so no gate protection resistor is needed. The circuit is thus simpler than for the BJT.

Figure **H** shows how the MOSFET is actually connected to make a transducer driver for the bell.

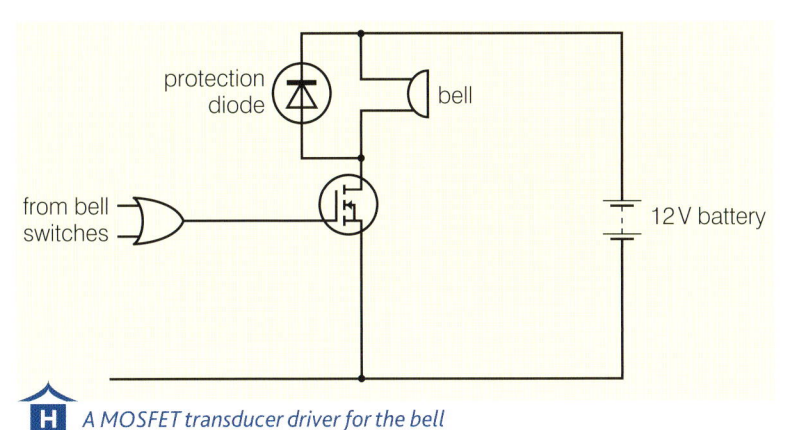

H *A MOSFET transducer driver for the bell*

> **AQA Examiner's tip**
>
> Transistors are examples of **active** devices. An active device is one which can provide power amplification. Passive devices cannot boost power. These include resistors, capacitors, diodes, relays, switches, the LDR and the thermistor.

BJT or MOSFET?

Since either type of transistor can be used as a transducer driver, why use one rather than the other? How do the differences between them affect our choice?

It is not just a case of using whichever one is the cheapest (although cost will probably come into it). There are some important characteristics of each type that you should use to help you make the right decision. These are best summarised in a table as shown in Table **I**.

Despite its problems, the MOSFET tends to be the transistor of choice for most of the things we do.

I *Comparing the BJT and the MOSFET*

characteristic	BJT	MOSFET
type of input signal needed to operate	**Current** This means that whatever is providing the input signal must be able to deliver enough current. This can be a problem for things like logic gates. The BJT, like a diode (see Chapter 11), needs at least 0.7 V at its input to work. The input signal will almost always be bigger than this, so it is not a problem in practice.	**Voltage** The voltage needed to turn on a MOSFET is about 2V. The input signal will almost always be more than this, so no problem there. Also, because the MOSFET doesn't draw any current at all from its input signal (we say that the MOSFET has a high input resistance), it can be successfully driven from logic gates, sensors etc.
peculiarities!	**No special problems** Provided that the currents and voltages that the BJT is working with are within its limits, it does what it says on the tin!	**Static sensitive** Like the BJT, the MOSFET must be used within its limits. In addition, it is also sensitive to static electricity at its gate. Because of this some MOSFETS can be damaged by excessive handling, and all MOSFETS can behave erratically if the gate is left unconnected (the technical name for the terminal of a component being left unconnected is **floating**).
efficiency	**High** The BJT does not waste a lot of power (get hot!) when it is used to turn something on and off.	**Low** Although it is not usually a problem in the sort of circuits we are dealing with, the MOSFET wastes quite a lot of power – it gets hot – when turning things on and off.

5.2 Transducer drivers using relay switches

The relay switch

The **relay** switch, unlike the transistor, has mechanical parts. It consists of an electromagnet (a solenoid), an iron armature and contacts. A typical relay is shown in Figure **A**.

The armature is normally held up by a spring, and so the contacts are apart from each other. When a current flows through the coil, the solenoid creates a magnetic field, and the iron armature is attracted to the core of the coil. This moves an insulating pin against the contacts, forcing them together. When the current is stopped, the magnetic field disappears, so the spring pulls the armature away and the contacts open.

A The relay switch

The circuit breaker, which we talked about in Chapter 1, works in a very similar way.

So, how does the relay work as a transducer driver? The current needed by the coil can be as low as 50 mA for some types, and the current that the contacts are able to switch on and off might be as high as 16 A; so, like the BJT, it is acting as a current 'booster'.

Where might it be used? A very common example is shown in Figure **B**. This is a relay that is used to operate the starter motor in a car when the ignition switch is operated.

B A relay switch for a car starter motor

When the ignition key is turned to the start position, you can often hear a 'clonk' just before the starter motor starts to turn the engine. This noise is from the relay. The small ignition switch connects the battery to the coil of the relay, and its contacts close, allowing current to pass through the starter motor. A relay is needed because the current drawn by the starter motor can be as high as 100 A, and there is no way that the ignition switch could handle this – it would melt!

One major advantage of the relay over the transistor is this. As the contacts are not linked electrically in any way to the coil (we say that the coil and the contacts are **isolated** from each other), the contacts can be used to switch high voltages on and off – like the domestic mains supply – with no risk of the components driving the coil being damaged.

Objectives

In this section you will learn:

- what a relay switch is, and how it works
- how to use the relay as a transducer driver
- how to compare the use of transistors and relay switches as transducer drivers.

Key terms

Relay: an electromechanical switch.

SPNO: (Single Pole, Normally Open). One of the common arrangement of relay contacts.

AQA Examiner's tip

It is important to remember the difference between the current that flows through the relay coil in order for the relay to operate, and the current that flows through the contacts. An example will illustrate this. A typical relay for switching the pump on and off in a domestic central heating system has a coil which requires 50 mA (0.05 A) to operate the electromagnet and close the contacts; this current is supplied by the transducer driver in the electronics. The pump runs at 240 V (the domestic mains supply) and requires 2 A, so 2 A will flow through the contacts when they are closed and the pump is on.

Other relay contact arrangements

Relays can actually have many more contacts than are shown in the previous example, and there are special names for all of them. If there is just one pair of contacts, the relay is called a **single-pole** (or SP) relay. If the contacts are open until the relay operates they are called **normally open** (NO) contacts, and if the contacts are closed until the relay operates, they are called **normally closed** (NC). The arrangement of contacts in the relay in the example is thus **SPNO**, and this is the simplest. There can, however, be a *pair* of switches that both close together, in which case it is called a **double-pole** (or DP) type. The relay can have a contact that moves *between* two other contacts, and then it becomes a **changeover** (CO) type.

Activity

Do some research to find out about all the different contact arrangements and their names (you will find that there is more than one name for some arrangements). Create a chart with diagrams showing all the contact arrangements you have found. Add to the chart pictures of some example relays that you have found, and give their coil and contact ratings.

The best of both worlds

You may have spotted the problem with using the relay instead of the transistor – the current needed by the coil is too big. Even the most sensitive of relays need a coil current of at least 50 mA to operate, and so we could not use the relay in our doorbell circuit in place of the BJT or the MOSFET. Neither would there be any reason to. Relays, being mechanical, are much less reliable than transistors, and would not do the job any better. But suppose that the doorbell system were to be used in a big warehouse, so that a very powerful, mains operated bell were needed. There is no way that a transistor would be able to switch the mains on and off; also it would not be wise to mix the mains up with our delicate logic circuit.

We can, however, use the transistor to turn on a relay, and then the relay to turn on the mains to the bell. This is shown in Figure **C**.

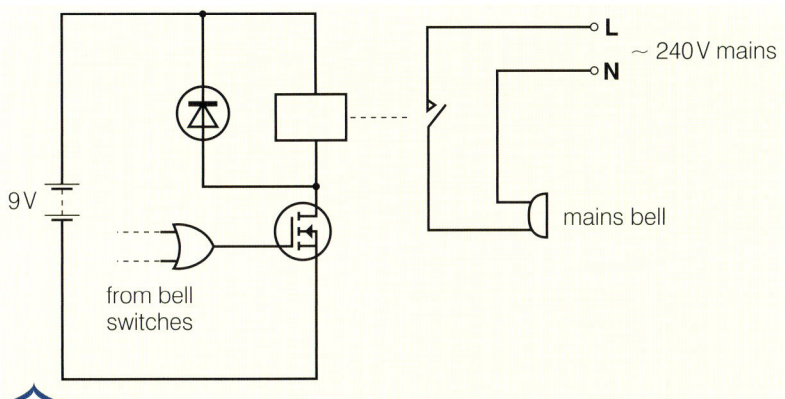

C *A bell circuit using a relay and a transistor*

Notice that a protection diode is now needed, as when we used the transistor to drive the bell directly, because of the relay coil.

(Please note that you should **not** try to build this yourself; the involvement of the mains makes it potentially very dangerous.)

⚭ links

Remind yourself why it would be dangerous to build this circuit by looking back at Chapter 1.

Something to think about...

In our doorbell example using the BJT, it was the current that was amplified in the transistor. When we used the MOSFET we said that no current at all is taken from the signal because the MOSFET has such a high input resistance. So, does a transducer driver boost the current, the voltage, or both?

There is no straightforward answer. In the doorbell example shown, the logic circuit works with a 12 V supply, and the bell is a 12 V type. So here it is the *current* that has to be boosted. Let us say we found a bell that *could* operate at a current of 2 mA, but needed a supply of 50 V. We would then have to boost the voltage.

You may have spotted that since power = voltage × current ($P = VI$), in both cases the *power* is the quantity that has to be boosted. Here is why.

The logic gate, operating at 12 V, can only manage to deliver a power of 12 V × 0.002 A, or 0.024 W (24 mW), whereas the 12 V, 0.5 A bell needs 12 × 0.5 or 6 W, and the 50 V, 2 mA bell needs 50 × 0.002 or 0.1 W.

This is true of most transducer drivers – they are really **power amplifiers**.

∞ **links**

There is more about power amplification in Chapter 10.

Summary

Electronic systems cannot usually drive transducers such as motors, lights, buzzers, etc. by themselves, and need a transducer driver to boost the power of the signal.

Transducer drivers can be made using a transistor or a relay.

The transistor can be a BJT (bipolar junction transistor) or a MOSFET type.

The BJT has the connections Base, Emitter and Collector; the MOSFET has the connections Gate, Source and Drain.

MOSFETS can be static sensitive, and the gate should not be left unconnected.

The MOSFET draws no current at its input (gate), so it is a good choice for use with logic gates.

The BJT requires a base resistor to limit the base current.

Transistors need a protection diode across the load if it is an electromagnetic device such as a motor, solenoid or relay.

The BJT is more efficient than the MOSFET (wastes less power).

The relay is an electromechanical device which, because it has isolation between the coil and the contacts, can be used to drive high voltage devices.

The simplest arrangement of relay contacts is SPNO (single pole, normally open).

The relay coil can be connected to a transistor to produce a transducer driver that will operate with small signals but that will switch a high voltage (like the 240 V mains).

Questions

1 a Explain why a transducer driver is often needed in an electronic system.
   b Describe the two main types of transducer driver.

2 A 12 V, 8 W motor is to be turned on by the signal from a logic system, and so a transducer driver is needed.
   a Draw the circuit diagram for a transducer driver based on a BJT, and label all components and connections.
   b Draw the circuit diagram for a transducer driver based on a MOSFET, and label all components and connections.
   c What will be the value of the collector current in the BJT when the motor is turned on?

3 An electronic engineer is designing a porch light, where a 60 W mains bulb is to be turned on by the signal from a light sensor. She decides to use a MOSFET and a relay for the transducer driver circuit. The supply to the electronic circuit is 9 V.
   a Why is it necessary to use a relay?
   b How much current should the contacts in the relay be able to carry?
   c Why is it necessary to have a protection diode across the relay coil?
   d Draw the full circuit diagram of the transducer driver, showing how it is connected to the bulb, and label all parts.

6 Making time delays

6.1 Capacitors

In all the circuits and systems looked at so far, everything happens instantly. In Chapter 2 the torch comes on the instant the button is pressed. Not only that, but the torch carries on working until it is stopped by releasing the button. Very often we need to either delay something turning on, or have something turn off automatically after a certain time has elapsed. One example where both of these things are wanted is in the kitchen timer, shown in Figure **A**.

A An electronic kitchen timer

The time can be selected by pressing the HRS and MIN buttons, and then pressing the START/STOP button. Nothing happens until the set period of time has elapsed, and then the buzzer turns on.

It would be irritating if it carried on buzzing forever, so 60 seconds after the buzzer has started, it is turned off automatically. Both of these actions require circuits that can produce time delays.

What is a capacitor?

In Chapter 3 we met resistors, probably one of the most important electronic components. The **capacitor** is another important component. It enables us to create circuits that produce time delays. For this reason it is worth looking at the capacitor in detail before looking at circuits that make use of it.

The capacitor is like an electricity 'bucket'. It fills up with electric charge when connected to a battery, and empties when you connect it to a circuit.

Figure **B** shows the circuit symbol for a capacitor, together with some pictures of typical capacitors that you will come across. The symbol actually gives a pretty good idea of how the capacitor is made. Essentially it is two metal plates separated by an insulating layer; for some types, the metal plates are long strips and are rolled up like a swiss roll, which is why some capacitors are tube-shaped.

> **Objectives**
>
> In this section you will learn:
>
> what a capacitor is and how it can be used to produce time delays
>
> to appreciate the difference between polarised and non-polarised capacitors, and know their symbols
>
> that the unit of capacitance is the farad
>
> how to interpret the markings on a capacitor.

> **Key terms**
>
> **Capacitor:** a component which stores electric charge.
>
> **Farad:** the unit of capacitance.
>
> **Working voltage:** the maximum voltage that a capacitor can withstand.

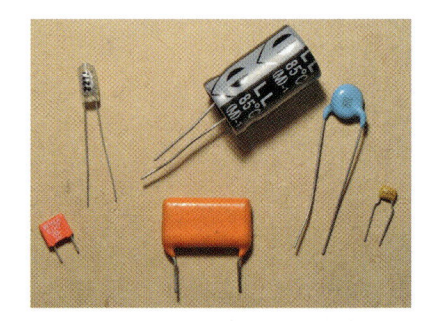

B The capacitor

Figure **C** shows what we mean by the 'bucket' idea. In (a), when the capacitor is connected across the battery, it **charges** ('fills up') very quickly. In (b) the capacitor has been disconnected from the battery, but it remains charged up. In theory, capacitors can stay like this forever; this is why we said in Chapter 1 that some pieces of electrical equipment can remain dangerous for some time after the mains supply has been disconnected. In practice, the charge does leak away inside the capacitor over a period of time. In (c) the capacitor is connected to a motor and **discharges** ('empties' its charge), causing the motor to turn.

Activity

1 Using a capacitor

Try this out! You will need a very large value of capacitor if the motor is to run for long enough to see the effect – at least 5 600 µF. You only need to touch the capacitor across the battery terminals very briefly. Make sure you connect it the right way round and that it has a high enough voltage rating (see later on).

C *Charging and discharging a capacitor*

Capacitance

The amount of charge that a capacitor is able to hold when connected to a given battery depends on its **capacitance**. The unit of capacitance is the **farad** (after Michael Faraday, the famous scientist). So, for the same voltage of battery a capacitor of 3 F will store three times as much charge as a capacitor of 1 F.

In practice, capacitors we usually use in electronics have values much smaller than 1 F, so we use fractions of farads instead. Table **D** shows all the different value sizes that you are likely to come across.

D *Different capacitor values*

value	F (farad)	µF (microfarad)	nF (nanofarad)	pF (picofarad)
1 F is the same thing as	1	1 000 000 (10^6)	1 000 000 000 (10^9)	1 000 000 000 000 (10^{12})
1 µF is the same thing as	0.000001 (10^{-6})	1	1000 (10^3)	1 000 000 (10^6)
1 nF is the same thing as	0.000000001 (10^{-9})	0.001 (10^{-3})	1	1000 (10^3)
1 pF is the same thing as	0.0000000000001 (10^{-12})	0.000001 (10^{-6})	0.001 (10^{-3})	1

In addition to their actual value, capacitors have a **working voltage**. Because of the way they are made, too high a voltage can cause the insulating layer between the plates to break down – electrons bash their way through it and the capacitor is usually permanently damaged. Make sure when you use a capacitor that its working voltage is greater than the voltage of the supply your circuit is using.

Electrolytic capacitors

One particular type of capacitor deserves a special mention, because it has to be treated with some care. The **electrolytic capacitor** is so called because the insulating layer between the plates is a chemical electrolyte (instead of being plastic or ceramic as many types are). Above about 1 μF most capacitors will be of this type; above 100 μF virtually all will be, because it is the only way such high values can be achieved.

The problem is that because of the electrolyte they are **polarised** – which means they have a positive (+) and a negative (−). It is essential that they are connected the right way round.

The symbol for an electrolytic capacitor is very similar to the non-electrolytic type. It is shown in Figure **F**, together with a photo of a typical electrolytic capacitor.

How do you know which way round to connect it? The (+) lead of an electrolytic capacitor is always the longer of the two. In addition, many have a black or grey stripe on the side of the (−) lead. The one in Figure **F** has both of these features.

Do not try it to connect the electrolytic capacitor the wrong way round. The electrolyte becomes a conductor rather than an insulator, the capacitor heats up and can explode, and clouds of nasty fumes can be given off.

The BS printed code for marking

Although most capacitors, especially the larger ones, have their values and working voltages marked on them, sometimes other means of indicating their values are used. In Chapter 3 the BS 1852 code for resistors was introduced, and this is also used for some capacitors, especially the smaller values and the tiny surface mounted types.

In this case, the value is given in pF (picofarads), but the same code system is used as for resistors. Figure **G** shows an example. In this case, the value is 221 J, which is 220 pF ± 5%.

Slowing down the charging up

Figure **C** showed a capacitor being charged up by connecting it across a battery. If instead of connecting the capacitor to the battery directly we include a resistor in the circuit, then the capacitor cannot charge up quickly. The resistor reduces the current flow and so slows the whole process down (like turning the tap almost off when filling up a bucket of water).

The result of this is that if the circuit is switched on and the voltage across the capacitor is measured with a multimeter, the voltage will gradually rise. This is shown in Figure **H**.

This arrangement is called an **RC circuit** (or sometimes **CR circuit**), and because it is the essential ingredient of all time delay circuits, you will meet it again and again.

The actual time that the capacitor takes to charge up depends upon the value of resistor and the value of capacitor.

Key terms

Electrolytic capacitor: a polarised capacitor.

Polarised: has a (+) and (−) connection.

RC circuit: a capacitor and a resistor connected together and used to produce time delays.

E Capacitor markings

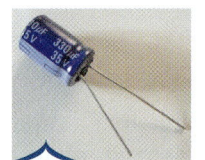

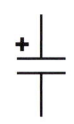

F The electrolytic capacitor

AQA Examiner's tip

If you are using electrolytic capacitors in your circuit, make absolutely sure before you switch on that you have connected them the right way round. If you haven't, then not only might you lose your circuit in a puff of smoke, you will also lose marks for not working safely!

G Using the BS printed code for capacitors

Chapter 6 Making time delays

If the value of resistor (in Ω) and the value of capacitor (in F) are multiplied together, the answer gives the number of seconds it will take for the voltage across the capacitor in the *RC* charging circuit to reach 63% of the battery voltage.

For example, if the battery is 9 V, *R* is 33 kΩ and *C* is 100 μF, then in a time of 33 000 × 100 × 0.000001 = 3.3 seconds the voltage across the capacitor will have reached 63% of 9 V or 5.7 V. You do not need to remember this, but it does help to explain how timing circuits actually work.

The fact that the capacitor in an *RC* circuit takes a definite and predictable time to charge up can be used to produce a time delay. All we need are a few extra bits and pieces.

> **AQA Examiner's tip**
> The value of $R \times C$ is called the **time constant** of the circuit. When you do this calculation, *R* must be in Ω and *C* in F.

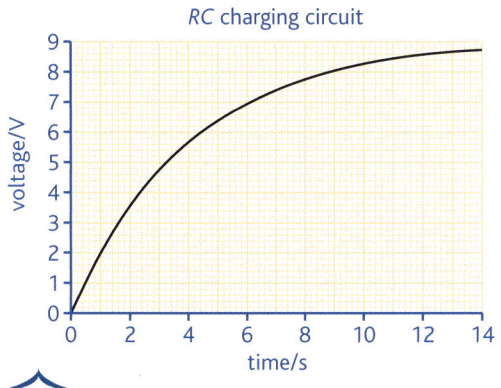

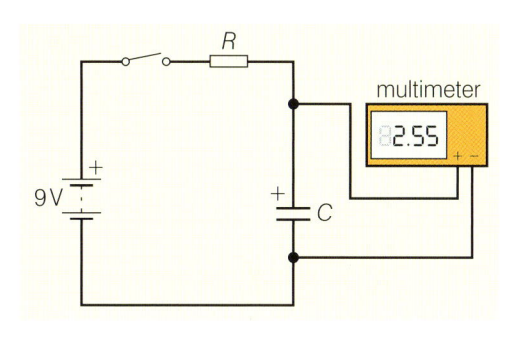

H The *RC* circuit

Activity

2 A time delay circuit

In Chapter 5 we introduced the transistor switch (when we used it as a transducer driver). A simple (but not very accurate) time delay circuit can be built using one of these together with an *RC* circuit.

The motor can be any sort, as long as it will run on a supply of 9 V.

You do not have to use the MOSFET suggested in Figure **I**. There are a huge range of types that will do the job.

Before you press the button there is no charge in the capacitor, so the voltage across it (and hence the voltage at the gate) will be zero – so the motor will be off.

Now press the button and keep it pressed. The capacitor will start charging through the resistor, so the voltage at the gate will start rising. Remember that the MOSFET switches on when the gate voltage is at about 2 V. So after some time has elapsed the gate will reach 2 V and the motor will come on.

I

What happens when you release the button? Can you explain this?

Discharge the capacitor by connecting a low value resistor across it (say 100 Ω). The motor should go off.

Turn off the supply, and swap the 1.2 MΩ resistor and the capacitor around (i.e. so that the capacitor is now connected between the switch and the supply, and the resistor between the gate and 0 V). Make sure that the capacitor is the right way round – its positive wire should be connected to the supply. Press the button and hold it on. How does the circuit behave now? Can you explain why? (This is tricky!)

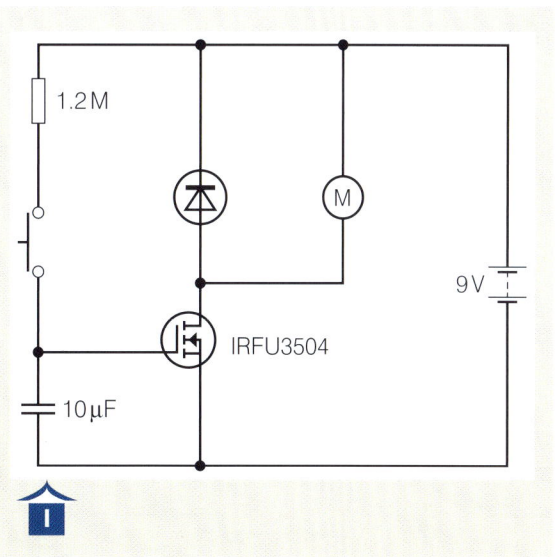

6.2 Time delay circuits

The 555 chip

In about 1971 a special chip was invented that could make use of the RC charging idea to produce time delays. The chip was named the **555** timer. Almost every electronic chip manufacturer now makes their own version of it – LM555 from National, NE555 from ST Microelectronics, MC1555 from Motorola etc. – and it is one of the most versatile and widely used chips around. Figure **A** shows the chip and its circuit symbol, with the names of all the pins identified.

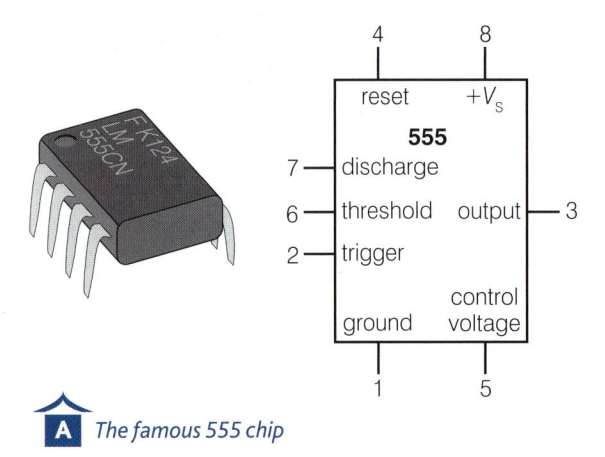

A The famous 555 chip

To make time delays, the 555 is connected to an *RC* charging circuit. Inside the chip is a comparing circuit which monitors the voltage across the capacitor (jump to Chapter 9 if you are desperate to know how this is done!), and a number of transistor switching circuits to control the charging process.

Figure **B** shows a circuit diagram of the 555 timer chip used to produce a time delay.

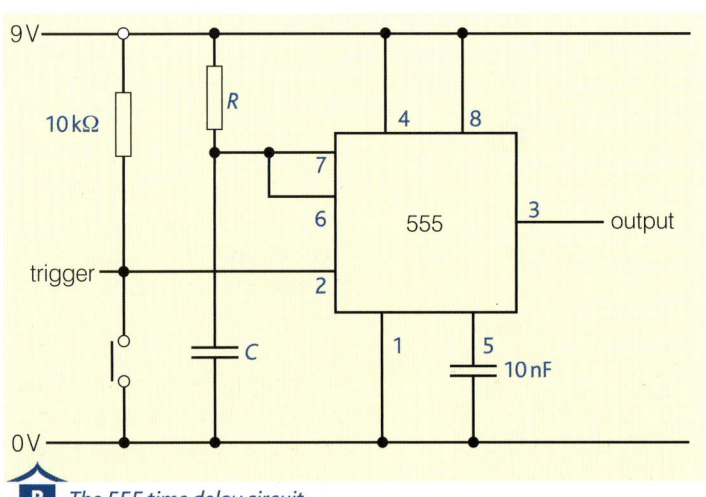

B The 555 time delay circuit

Objectives

In this section you will learn:

what a monostable is, what it does and what it can be used for

how the 555 timer chip works

the names of the inputs and outputs of the chip

to recognise and reproduce the circuit diagram of a 555 monostable circuit

how the 555 monostable circuit is triggered and the requirements for the trigger signal

how to calculate the values of components in a monostable circuit to produce a given time period.

AQA Examiner's tip

Students often get very confused about the pin numbering. The thing to remember is that the circuit diagram, or the symbol of the chip (as shown in Figure **A**), has the connections laid out in an order that makes the diagram logical and neat, with the inputs on the left, the output on the right and the power supply and 0 V top and bottom, respectively. This does not follow the order in which the chip itself has its pins – these are numbered consecutively, in an anti-clockwise direction round the chip.

Chapter 6 Making time delays

The **trigger** is the signal that starts the whole thing off. When the trigger signal is taken to 0 V momentarily a transistor switch in the 555 turns the output on. The capacitor C then starts charging through resistor R. When the voltage across it has reached two-thirds of the supply voltage, the output is turned off. Another transistor switch is then connected across the capacitor, which discharges it through the discharge pin. This circuit is called a **monostable**.

Now is a good time to use a timing diagram to show how the trigger signal relates to the 555 output signal (look back over Chapter 3 to remind yourself about these), and this is shown in Figure **C**.

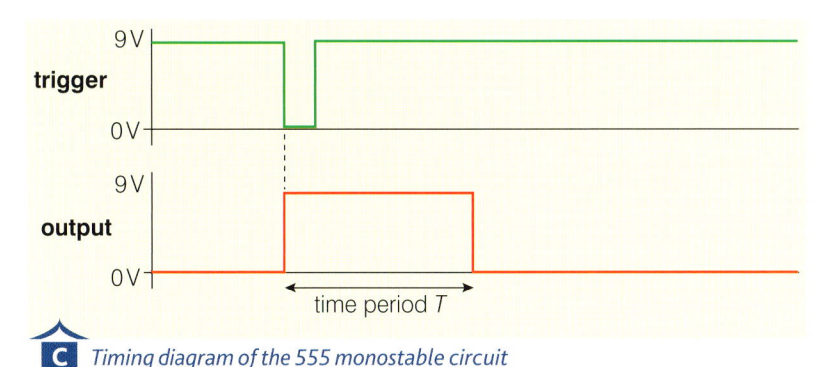

C Timing diagram of the 555 monostable circuit

> **Key terms**
> **555:** the 555 timer integrated circuit.
> **Trigger:** the signal (and name of the pin) that starts the 555 timing period.
> **Monostable:** the technical name for the 555 time delay circuit.

> **AQA Examiner's tip**
> You need to be able to recognise the 555 diagram, and the names of its pins. Questions will often be asked that require you to complete the circuit diagram of the monostable circuit; so you need to know how all the different pins and the components are connected.

Calculating the monostable period

The time for which the output is on (or **high**) is called the time period. As you might expect, the calculation involves multiplying the value of R by the value of C.

$$T = 1.1 \times R \times C \text{ (seconds)}$$

As an example, if R were 5.6 kΩ and C were 47 μF, the time period would be

$$1.1 \times 5600 \times 47 \times 10^{-6} = 0.263 \text{ s}$$

(or 263 ms – just over a quarter of a second).

Now we have a circuit that can produce an accurate time delay, on demand. The range of time delays possible with the 555 monostable circuit is impressive. The shortest is about 1 μs (1 millionth of a second) and the longest about 5 minutes.

Can *any* values of R and C be used? The circuit will work with most values of capacitor. There are however limits to the values of resistor. If R is less than about 1 kΩ too much current flows when the 555 switches. If R is more than 5.6 MΩ too little current flows for it to work properly. Stick to values of resistor well within this range.

> **AQA Examiner's tip**
> Remember that in the formula R must be in Ω and C in F.

> **AQA Examiner's tip**
> You will not be asked to explain how the 555 chip works – but you must know how the monostable is triggered, what the output then does, and how to do the calculation for the time period!

What are the other resistor and capacitor for?

It is important to remember that the 555 monostable is spurred into action when the trigger input drops to 0 V. We say that the chip is **falling edge triggered.** This means that in the absence of a trigger signal the trigger input has to be held high. A pull-up resistor is used. Without it the trigger input would 'float' and the circuit would not work. The value of the pull-up resistor does not matter too much – 10 kΩ is usual.

> **AQA Examiner's tip**
> You must remember that the trigger of the 555 has to be taken from high to low to start the timing period. It is worth knowing that if the trigger input is kept low the timing period carries on – the output stays high. Many projects have not worked because of this problem.

The other capacitor is for noise or interference suppression. Dodgy signals picked up by pin 5 can cause the chip to misbehave. Nine times out of ten the circuit *will* work without it, but it is good practice to always have it there. Its value is not critical, and you will find that 10 nF is a very popular choice.

> **links**
>
> Chapter 4 looks at the idea of pull-up resistors.

Making a signal come on after a given delay

You will have spotted that this monostable circuit produces a signal that comes on straight away and goes *off* after the specified delay. As mentioned earlier, sometimes this is what is needed, but sometimes a circuit is needed that switches *on* after a period of time. Figure **D** shows how this can be achieved.

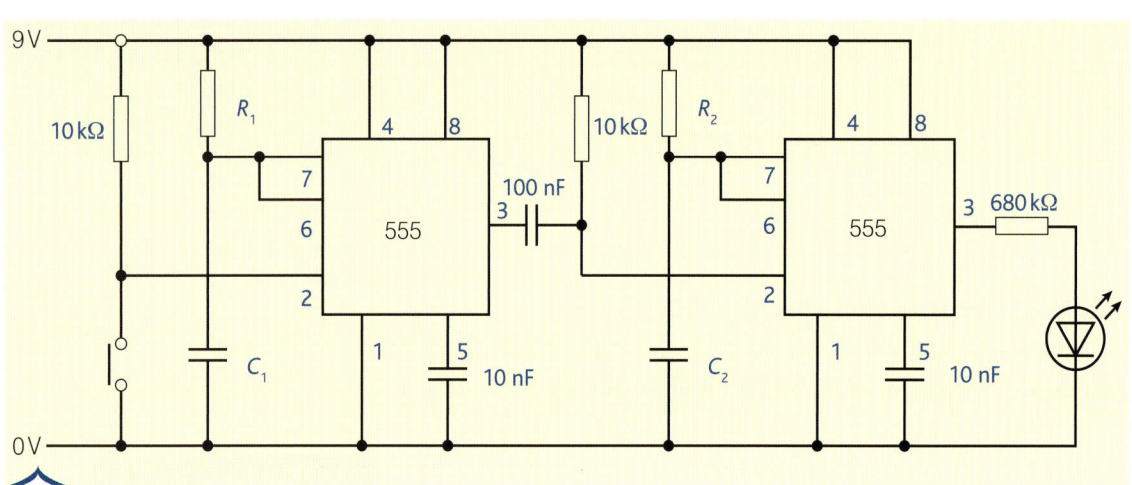

D Using two 555s to make a signal come on after a delay

This circuit is shown with a push-button switch to trigger it, and an LED as the output.

When the button is pressed and released, the first 555 monostable turns its output on. This does not affect the second 555 monostable, because its trigger has to go from high to low to start it timing. After a time period determined by R_1 and C_1 the first 555 turns its output off. This triggers the second 555 which thus starts timing, and the LED will come on. After the time period specified by R_2 and C_2 the LED will go off.

The capacitor linking the output of the first 555 to the trigger of the second is essential. It ensures that only the change from high to low gets passed through – otherwise the second time period would never stop!

> **AQA Examiner's tip**
>
> Sometimes circuits using 555s suffer from noise on the power supply rails, causing random behaviour. This can be cured by putting capacitors across the power supply.

The dual timer

A very useful chip is the 556. This is a 14-pin device that contains two independent 555s.

Chapter 6 Making time delays

Summary

When connected across a battery a capacitor charges up (stores electric charge).

An electrolytic capacitor is a type of capacitor which must only be connected one way round in a circuit, and that it is the usual type for values above about 1 µF.

You have learnt how to read and interpret the markings on a capacitor.

By connecting a capacitor to a supply via a resistor it can be made to charge up slowly, thereby forming the basic time delay circuit.

The 555 chip is a special timer integrated circuit, containing switches and comparing circuits.

The 555 can be used with an *RC* circuit to produce time delays, and is called a monostable.

You should now be able to recognise the circuit diagram of the 555 monostable.

You should be able to describe the operation of the 555 monostable.

The time period of a 555 monostable, or the component values needed for a desired time period can be calculated using

$$T = 1.1R \times C \text{ (seconds)}.$$

Questions

1 On the right is a partly drawn circuit diagram of a 555 monostable.
   a Copy out and add the connections necessary to complete the diagram.
   b Fully label all inputs and outputs.
   c Explain how the circuit behaves when the push button switch is pressed.

2 A monostable is to be used to create a time delay of 40 s for the timer in a porch light.
   a Choose suitable values for the timing components.
   b How could the time delay be made easily adjustable?

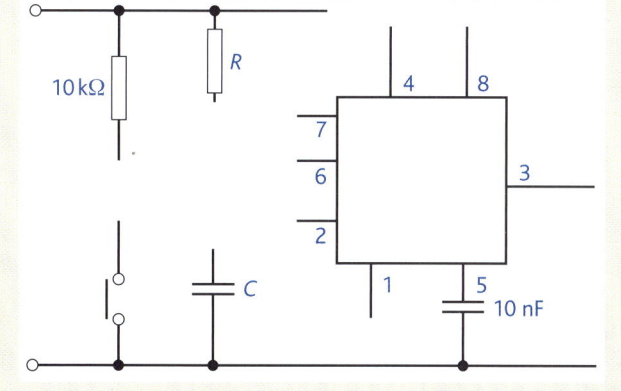

3 You are designing a 555 monostable timer which is to have a period of 66 ms. You have available a 10 µF capacitor.
   a Calculate the value of resistor required.
   b What would the time delay actually be if the nearest preferred value of resistor were used?

7 Making continuous pulses

7.1 Uses of continuous pulses

So far you have been looking at signals that go on and stay on (like in the torch) or that go on for a fixed period of time and then turn off (like the buzzer on a kitchen timer). In many electronic systems a signal is needed that goes on and off continuously. There are two main uses for this, which are best explained by giving a couple of examples.

■ Flashing and buzzing

When your alarm clock goes off first thing in the morning it needs to attract your attention to wake you up. A 'beep, beep, beep' noise is more likely to do this than a continuous buzz. So most alarm clocks have a circuit in them which, when started, continuously turns a signal on and off, and this is connected to a buzzer (via a transducer driver).

When your mobile phone is plugged into its charger it almost certainly has a little light that flashes on and off to tell you that it is busy charging its battery. When it is finished (fully charged) the light goes off.

Both of these examples show the use of a signal that goes on and off all the time: both to attract attention, one audibly the other visually. The rate at which the signal goes on and off is not crucial, and is decided purely by what sounds or looks right.

■ Clocks and watches

Most people's watches these days are electronic. Apart from sports watches, they usually show the time to the nearest second, and even the cheapest ones do this to an accuracy of just a few seconds in a month. How can they do this? They have a circuit which generates a signal that goes on then off, repeatedly, at a rate of exactly once per second. It then has a special circuit which counts up by one every time the signal goes on, and shows the accumulated count on a display. Actually it's a bit more complicated than that! For one thing, it has to work out the minutes and hours and display those as well. It is still however based on the simple idea of generating a continuous stream of ons and offs, and counting them.

A computer performs millions of different operations every second, and these all have to be done one at a time in the correct sequence. Just as an orchestra needs a conductor to keep everything in step, a computer needs some sort of timing device. A continuous on/off signal is used to do this, and, rather confusingly, is known as a **clock**. (Chapter 13 looks at the microcontroller, and here you will learn more about this idea.)

Unlike with the flashers and buzzers, for both these examples it really matters what the precise on/off rate is. In the case of the watch it has to be *exactly* once per second; in the computer it will be something like 3 000 000 000 times per second!

Objectives

In this section you will learn:

about the uses of continuous pulses.

links

Chapter 8 looks at the special circuits and devices that form the counters.

Chapter 7 Making continuous pulses

7.2 Generating the signal

Before looking at the actual circuits that can make a continuous on/off signal, it is helpful to look at this type of signal in a bit more detail.

Figure **A** shows a typical on/off signal with the important characteristics identified.

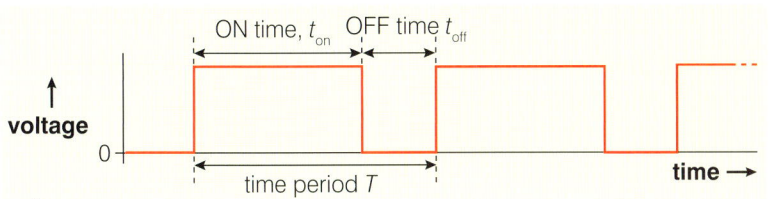

A *A periodic signal*

Signals like this - that have a regular repeated pattern - are called **periodic signals**. The time the signal takes before it repeats its shape is called the **time period**, and this is made up of the **on time** and the **off time**. Very often the 'on' bits are referred to as **pulses**, and the whole thing referred to as a **pulse train** or **pulse waveform**.

In many systems the *rate* at which the signal turns on and off is more important than the individual on and off times. The rate at which a periodic signal repeats is called the **frequency**, and this is of course related to the period. The frequency is measured in **hertz** (after Heinrich Hertz, another famous scientist), and is usually abbreviated to **Hz**. If, for example, the time period were 0.2 seconds, then you would be able to fit five repeats into one second – in other words the frequency would be 5 Hz.

So the formula for this is:

$$f = \frac{1}{T} \text{Hz}$$

where f = frequency and T = time period in seconds.

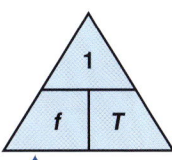

B *Formula triangle for frequency and time period*

Objectives

In this section you will learn:

what a periodic signal is

that the unit of frequency is hertz (Hz), and how frequency is related to time period

the difference between on time, off time and time period.

Key terms

On time: the time for which a periodic signal is high.

Off time: the time for which a periodic signal is low.

Pulse: a signal which goes high for a certain time and then goes low again; a pulse train is a continuous stream of pulses.

Frequency: the rate at which a periodic signal repeats.

Activity

If you look at the back of a television, radio or hi-fi (make sure you switch it off at the mains first), you will usually find a label giving details like serial number, model number and so-on. In addition, it will say something like '220–240 V, 50 Hz'. This indicates that it is designed to operate on the UK mains supply, which has a voltage of around about 230 V and a frequency of 50 Hz. So the mains voltage must have a shape that repeats itself – i.e. it is periodic. Re-arrange the formula above, and use it to work out what the time period of the mains voltage is. When you get to Chapter 11 you will learn more about the 'shape' of the mains voltage supply.

7.3 Making the pulses

So, what circuit can be used to generate a continuous on/off signal – a train of pulses? You will sometimes see the circuits that can do this referred to as 'continuous pulse producers'. Although this does explain what they do, it is more usual to call them **pulse generators**. There is also a proper technical name for it. It is called an **astable** (pronounced 'ay-stable').

There are quite a few circuits that can be used to make an astable; but one device that can do it has only just been introduced to you – the 555 timer chip.

To make continuous pulses the 555 has to be connected to an RC charging circuit, as before, but this time the circuit connections are slightly different, because the chip has to 're-start itself' after producing each pulse. Figure **A** shows the arrangement.

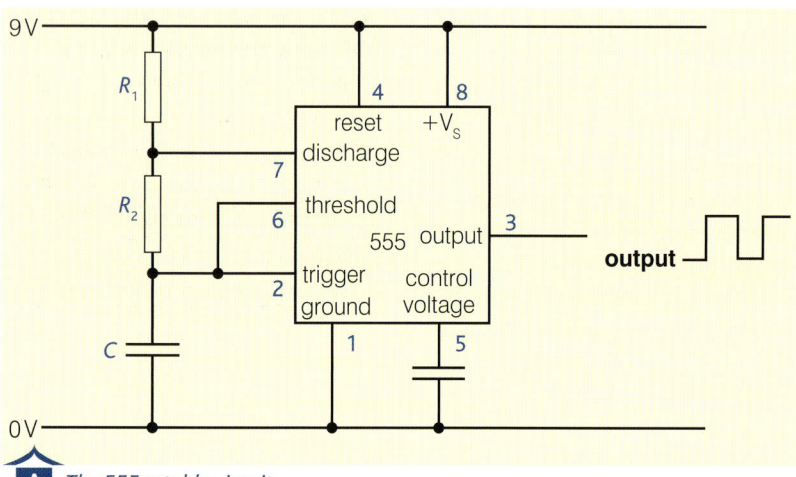

Objectives

In this section you will learn:

what an astable is, what it does and what it can be used for

how the 555 timer chip works in astable mode

to recognise and reproduce the diagram of a 555 astable circuit

how to calculate the values of components needed in a 555 astable circuit in order to produce a signal with a given time period or frequency.

Key terms

Pulse generator: a common name for the astable.

Astable: a circuit which generates a continuous on/off signal or pulse train.

A The 555 astable circuit

When power is first applied the output goes high, because the trigger is low. C starts to charge up, but this time through R_1 and R_2. As before, when it reaches about two-thirds of the supply voltage the output turns off (because this is the function of the threshold pin). A switch inside the 555 then connects pin 7 to 0 V, and so the capacitor starts to discharge, but through R_2 only. When it reaches one-third of the supply voltage the output turns on again. Because the trigger (pin 2) is this time connected to pin 6, the 555 keeps itself going, without the need for an input signal to start it off. So the whole cycle then starts again, and repeats until the power is turned off.

As you might expect, the maths that relates the values of the timing components to the time periods of the output signal is a bit more complicated than for the monostable in Chapter 6.

the ON time, in seconds, is given by: $t_{on} = 0.7(R_1 + R_2)C$
and the OFF time, in seconds, is given by: $t_{off} = 0.7R_2C$

R must be in ohms and C in farads.

Something really important to note about these equations is that they show that the off time will always be shorter than the on time.

Chapter 7 Making continuous pulses 57

The time period of the output signal is the sum of the on and off times. If you add the two formulae together you get this:

time period, in seconds: $T = \dfrac{(R_1 + 2R_2)C}{1.44}$

Finally, if you use the formula triangle you can rearrange this to give you the frequency of the signal:

frequency, in Hz: $f = \dfrac{1.44}{(R_1 + 2R_2)C}$

A worked example

Look at the astable circuit in Figure **B**. All the component values are shown, so we can work out the frequency of the pulses it produces.

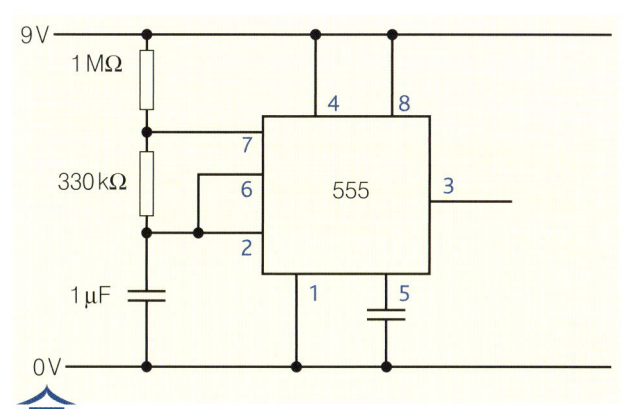

B *The 555 astable circuit with component values*

The frequency of the signal from this astable will be given by:

$$f = \dfrac{1.44}{(R_1 + 2R_2)C}$$

$$= \dfrac{1.44}{(1\,000\,000 + 2 \times 330\,000) \times 0.000001} \text{ Hz}$$

Although this is perfectly correct, it is *really* easy to make mistakes because of the huge number of zeros you have to remember to put in. It is much better to use scientific notation; the formula then looks like this:

$$= \dfrac{1.44}{(1 \times 10^6 + 2 \times 330 \times 10^3) \times 1 \times 10^{-6}} \text{ Hz}$$

$$\approx 87 \text{ Hz}$$

($\approx$ means 'approximately equal to'. The *actual* answer – the one your calculator will give you – is 86.7 Hz.)

We can use the formula triangle shown in Topic 7.2 to work out what the time period of the wave is:

$$T = \dfrac{1}{f} \text{ seconds}$$

so $T = \dfrac{1}{87}$ s

or 0.0115 s (11.5 ms)

AQA Examiner's tip

You do not need to remember all of these formulae. You could however be asked to work out the period, and the formula will be given to you. You will be given the formula that relates time period to frequency as well.
It is, though, always a good idea to try and remember as many formulae as you can; it speeds up your work, and remembering them by practising using them is a great way to increase your understanding.

AQA Examiner's tip

You need to be able to recognise the 555 chip diagram, and the names of its pins. Questions will often be asked that require you to complete the circuit diagram of the astable circuit; so you need to know how all the different pins and the components are connected.

AQA Examiner's tip

As with the monostable, you need to remember that in the formulae R must be in ohms, and C must be in farads. If you always make sure you convert your resistor and capacitor values first before putting them into the equation then you shouldn't go wrong. Also, it is better to work out the formula in small bites. For instance, in the example above it's safer to calculate $2 \times R_2$ first, then add R_1 to your answer, then multiply this answer by C, and then finally calculate 1.44 divided by your answer. If you try and tap it all into your calculator in one go you may make a mistake.

Activity

Here is a very good application of the 555 astable to try out. The circuit in Figure **C** below is a 'heads-and-tails' indicator, with a red LED representing heads and a green LED representing tails. When the button is pressed, the LEDs flash alternately as the output of the 555 goes high and then low. The values of components have been chosen so that this happens very quickly, too fast to see. When the button is released, the connection from the RC circuit to the 555 is broken, and it stops in whatever state it was in at the time. It is anybody's guess whether this will be high or low, so which LED is on is effectively random.

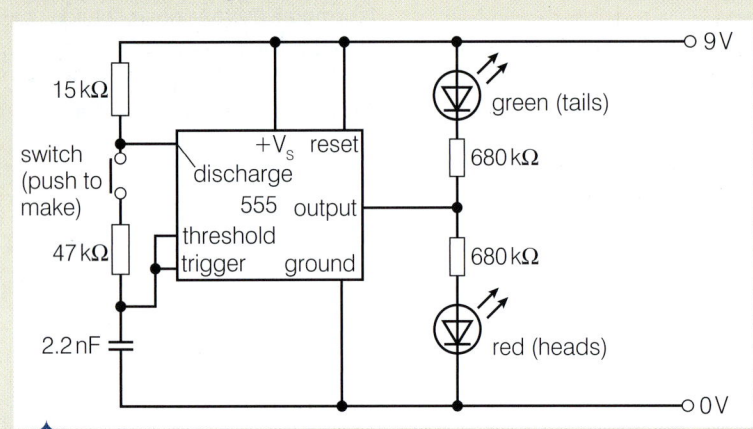

C A heads-and-tails indicator circuit

When you've built it, see if you can answer these questions about how it works:

a What are the 680 Ω resistors for? (Chapter 3 will help).
b What frequency does the astable run at?
c Why do the LEDs come on alternately?
d Which LED comes on when the 555 output is low?

7.4 Checking for a pulse

■ Hearing it

How can we tell if any pulses are actually coming out of the 555 astable? Are they what we wanted? How do we know that our calculations were correct?

In the activity in Topic 7.3, LEDs were used as outputs of the 555, and if the pulses are slow enough, connecting an LED (and a series resistor – see Chapter 3 to remind you why) to the output will confirm that the pulses are there – the LED will go on and off. What if the pulses are too fast for this?

Right at the start of the chapter we talked about continuous pulses being needed for the buzzer in an alarm clock. In this sort of system the obvious way to find out if the pulses are right is to listen to them.

■ The loudspeaker

What we need is an **output transducer** which will convert the electrical pulses into sound. The most common way of doing this is to use a loudspeaker. Few people will have managed to avoid hearing a loudspeaker at some time or other, as loudspeakers are used in radios, hi-fi systems and televisions to produce the sound (you will learn more about these sorts of systems in Chapters 10 and 12). However, not everyone knows what a loudspeaker looks like or how it works.

A typical loudspeaker is shown in Figure **A**, together with a diagram showing how it is constructed.

Objectives

In this section you will learn:

what a loudspeaker is, and how to use it as an output transducer

what an oscilloscope is, and how to use it to show and measure a periodic signal.

Key terms

Loudspeaker: a transducer that converts an electrical signal into sound.

Oscilloscope: an instrument that will display the picture of a changing signal.

∞ links

You learned about output transducers in Chapter 5.

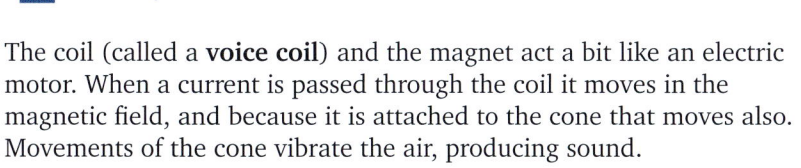

A *The loudspeaker*

The coil (called a **voice coil**) and the magnet act a bit like an electric motor. When a current is passed through the coil it moves in the magnetic field, and because it is attached to the cone that moves also. Movements of the cone vibrate the air, producing sound.

Loudspeakers come in all shapes and sizes, from tiny printed circuit board (PCB)-mounted devices of 20 mm diameter or less, to huge units of 40 cm diameter or more! It just depends how much sound you want.

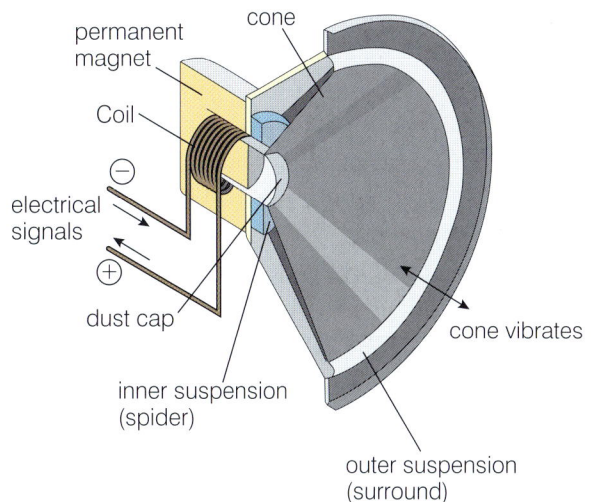

In practice the loudspeaker is built into a cabinet, or into the case of the appliance.

All we need to do then is to connect the output of the 555 to a loudspeaker, as shown in Figure **B**.

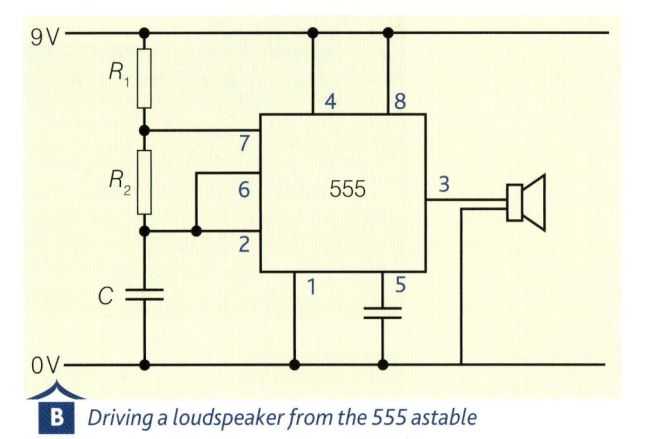

B *Driving a loudspeaker from the 555 astable*

The voice coil in a loudspeaker usually has a resistance of 8 Ω, but you can get them with resistances of 16 Ω, and small ones with coils of 32 Ω and 64 Ω.

The 555 won't be able to drive an 8 Ω device, and one with a resistance of 64 Ω would be suitable. Even with this, doesn't the 555 need a transducer driver? No – the 555 effectively has a transducer driver built-in. (See Chapter 5 if you need to remind yourself what transducer drivers are).

Seeing it

The pulses may be so fast that we wouldn't be able to hear them; in which case, using a loudspeaker would not work. Furthermore, we may want to see *exactly* what the shapes of the pulses are – for example, what the on and off times are. Finally we may want to actually measure the period of the signal.

We can do all this using a special piece of test equipment whose full name is cathode ray oscilloscope. Generally it is referred to as an **oscilloscope**, or simply 'scope'. It is also quite common to use the abbreviation for it – CRO.

Figure **C** is a picture of one of hundreds of different types of oscilloscope, but they are all very similar in what they do and how you use them.

Although you do not need to know *how* the oscilloscope works, knowing a little bit about it will help you to understand how to set it up and use it.

The heart of the oscilloscope is the cathode ray tube (or CRT). This is a large glass tube with a vacuum inside.

Figure **D** shows a picture of the actual CRT removed from an oscilloscope, and above it a diagram showing what the inside of the tube consists of.

Electrons are produced by the electron 'gun', and these travel down the tube, striking the face at the right-hand end. A coating on the inside of the face turns the electron's energy into light, and so you get a bright dot of light where it hits the face. The clever part is being able to bend – or deflect – the electron beam so it hits the face wherever we want

AQA Examiner's tip

There are two types of 555 in common use. One is the standard type, and one – called a 7555 – is a low current device. The 7555 device cannot drive a loudspeaker, not even a 64 Ω one. So it would not work in the circuit in Figure B. It cannot even produce enough current at its output to drive the reset pin of another 555. Only consider the 7555 if you really must limit the power consumption of your system.

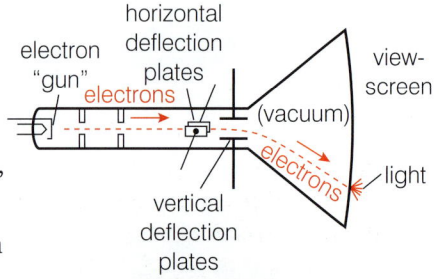

C *An oscilloscope*

D *The cathode ray tube*

Chapter 7 Making continuous pulses

it to. This is done using **deflection plates**. There are two sets of these; one set to move the dot from left to right (the X direction), and one set to move it up and down (the Y direction).

The signal you want to look at is applied to the vertical (Y) plates, so the dot will move up and down in sympathy with the signal. The oscilloscope itself drives the dot from left to right, repeatedly. So, what the oscilloscope does, in effect, is to draw a timing diagram of the signal on its screen.

The screen is marked in centimetre squares – like graph paper – so that measurements can be made.

The display on the screen for the worked example shown in Topic 7.3, Figure **B**, the 87 Hz astable, would look a bit like Figure **E**:

From the **trace** (the picture drawn on the screen) you can measure the period and the **amplitude**, in centimetres. The period should be measured in seconds and the amplitude in volts. The oscilloscope has controls that can be set to make it take a precise number of volts to make it go up vertically, and a precise amount of time to travel across horizontally. These two controls are called the **vertical sensitivity (Y-sensitivity)** and the **timebase**, respectively.

Although all oscilloscopes look slightly different, these two controls are always there, and always do the same thing. Figure **F** shows what the controls typically look like, and it shows clearly how they would have to be set to give the trace shown in Figure **E**.

Once you have measured the period, you can then calculate the **frequency**.

The oscilloscope is one of the most important and useful pieces of test equipment in the electronics laboratory.

> **Key terms**
>
> **Amplitude:** the size of a periodic signal.
>
> **Vertical sensitivity (Y-sensitivity):** the number of volts that are needed to move the oscilloscope trace up by 1 cm.
>
> **Timebase:** the number of seconds each cm represents across the oscilloscope screen.
>
> **Frequency:** the rate at which a periodic signal repeats – expressed in Hz (hertz).

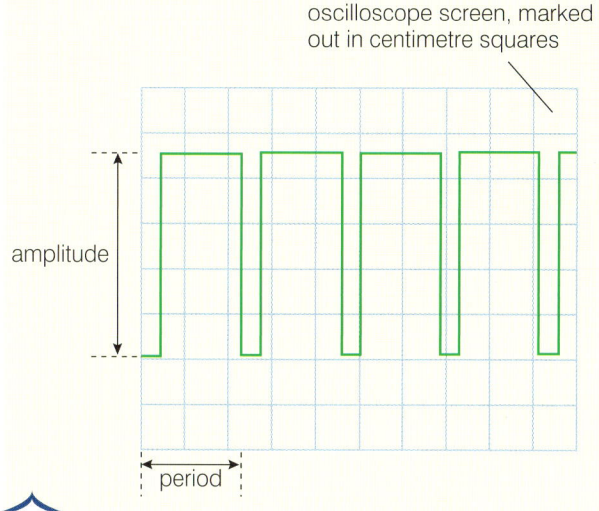

E *The display of the 87 Hz astable signal on the oscilloscope screen*

Activity

1 Using the oscilloscope

You can very easily show a periodic signal on the oscilloscope without having to build an astable. Set the vertical sensitivity to about 0.5 V/div and the timebase to about 5 ms/div. Adjust the vertical position control until the trace is in the middle of the screen. Connect up an input lead to the oscilloscope, and hold the positive wire (or the probe tip) in one hand (do not touch the negative wire). If you have set up your oscilloscope properly you should see a periodic signal appear on the screen. You may need to fiddle with the controls to get it to fit on the screen and to be stable (get help from your teacher with this). What you are seeing is not a heartbeat or anything else from your body, but a signal picked up from the mains electricity wiring around the room – your body is acting as an aerial. Prove this by moving your other hand near to the power cable of something that is plugged into the mains – the signal should get a lot bigger.

Measure the time period of the signal from the screen, and from this calculate its frequency. Does your answer sound familiar?

VOLTS/DIV

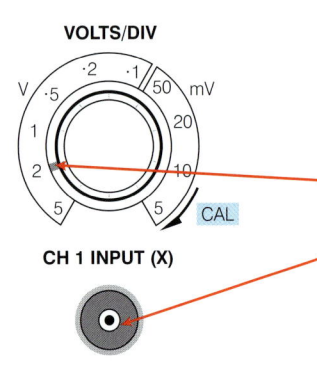

This is a view of the front panel of an oscilloscope, showing the vertical control or vertical sensitivity. It is called 'VOLTS/DIV' which means voltage per division – the word division is often used to mean 1 cm. It is marked in V (volts) and mV (millivolts).

It is set to 2 V per division, which means that every 1 cm vertically represents 2 volts, so the amplitude of signal in figure **E** is 4.5 divisions × 2 V = 5 V

CH 1 INPUT (X)

Into this socket you plug a cable that is connected to the signal you want to look at.

TIME/DIV

This shows the horizontal control or timebase. It is called TIME/DIV which means time per division. It is marked in s (seconds), ms (milliseconds) and μs (microseconds).

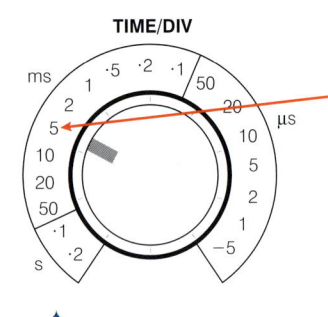

It is set to 5 ms per division, which means that the period of the signal in Figure **E** is 2.25 divisions × 5 ms = 11.25 ms (0.01125 s) Using the formula triangle for frequency and time, the frequency in figure **E** is $\frac{1}{0.01125} = 89$ Hz

F Oscilloscope controls set to display the signal

■ What does the 'reset' pin on the 555 chip do?

The reset pin was not mentioned in the last chapter, because it is not really used that much with the 555 in monostable mode. When using the 555 as an astable it can be very useful.

When the reset pin is at the supply voltage, the 555 operates as normal. When it is at 0 V the 555 is turned off, and its output is at 0 V (low).

Activity

2 The astable

Here is a fun system to build, which makes use of the 555's reset pin. Design and build an astable that runs at 400 Hz, and one that runs at 2 Hz. Connect the output from the 2 Hz astable to the reset pin of the 400 Hz astable (instead of the reset pin going to +supply as normal). The 400 Hz astable will then be turned on and off at a rate of 2 Hz. Connect the output of the 400 Hz astable to a loudspeaker.

Once you have tried it out, have a go at these questions:
  a Can you predict what the sound will be like?
  b Draw the timing diagram for the signal that feeds the loudspeaker
  c Look at the signal on the oscilloscope. Does it look like your diagram?
  d Change the frequencies of both astables to get a range of sounds
  e What will happen if you connect the astables the other way round (i.e. the 400 Hz astable drives the reset pin of the 2 Hz astable, and the loudspeaker is connected to the output of the 2 Hz astable)? Can you explain this?

AQA Examiner's tip

The 7555 (low current version of 555) cannot produce enough current at its output to drive the reset pin of another 7555. So you have to use the ordinary 555 in this activity. As before, the advice is to stick to the standard 555 for all your circuits.

Chapter 7 Making continuous pulses

Summary

Some systems need a signal that continuously goes on and off.

A continuous on/off signal is called a periodic signal.

The time for one repeat of a periodic signal is called the time period, and this consists of the on time (time for which the signal is high) and the off time (time for which the signal is low).

The frequency of a periodic signal is the rate at which it repeats, equal to 1/time period.

The frequency is measured in Hz.

A circuit which generates continuous on/off signals is called an astable or pulse generator.

You should be able to recognise the circuit arrangement for the 555 astable.

You should be able to use the reset pin of the 555 to start and stop the astable.

A loudspeaker is a transducer that converts an electrical signal into sound.

The loudspeaker can be used with the 555 astable so that its output signal can be heard.

An oscilloscope can be used to show the shape of a changing (especially periodic) signal.

The oscilloscope can be used to measure the amplitude and time period of a periodic signal.

Questions

1. Which of the following signals are periodic? Explain your answers.
   a. The signal from the water level sensor used in a washing machine
   b. The domestic mains supply
   c. The signal that drives the blue light on an ambulance
   d. The signal from a light sensor on a street lamp
   e. The ring tone on a mobile phone (discuss!)
   f. The signal that drives the reversing alarm on a lorry or van

2. The frequency of a signal is 150 Hz. What is its time period?

3. This figure shows an incomplete circuit diagram of a 555 astable. Complete the diagram by adding the missing components and connections, and fill in the missing pin labels.

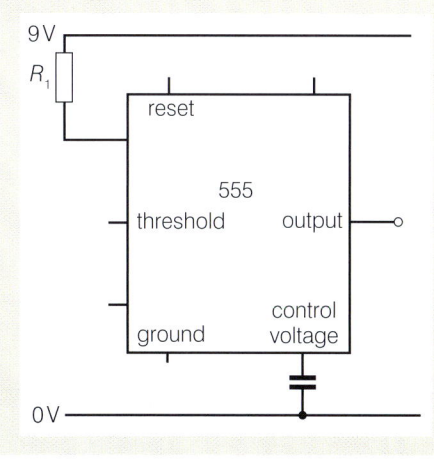

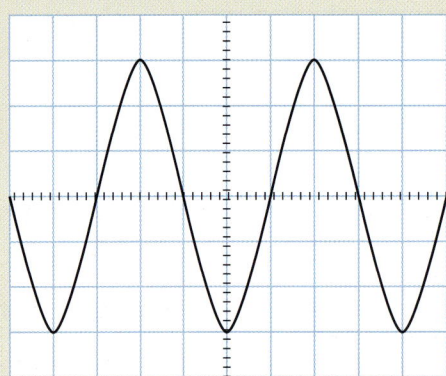

4 A student connects a signal generator to an oscilloscope, and the following trace was produced:

The Y-sensitivity is set to 0.1 V per division and the timebase is set to 2 ms per division.
- a Calculate the period of the signal.
- b Calculate the frequency of the signal.
- c What is the amplitude of the signal?
- d What is the name for a wave of this shape?

8 Latching and counting circuits

8.1 Counting circuits

Counting is very important in electronics. Electronic counters are used in a car park to tell drivers when the car park is full or for a chemist counting tablets when preparing a prescription to give the patient the correct number of tablets. Digital clocks and stopwatches both use counters; they count seconds, minutes and hours produced by an accurate **astable**.

The 4017

The 4017 is a counter that counts from 0 to 9. The 4017 counts pulses at the clock input. Every time the signal at the clock input changes from 0 to 1 the count increases and the next LED glows. If the counter starts with the LED 0 glowing, after one pulse LED 1 will glow and all the others will be off, and after two pulses LED 2 will glow. This continues until the ninth pulse which makes LED 9 glow. On the tenth pulse the counter resets and LED 0 glows again. The 0 to 1 signal which makes the counter count is called a **rising edge** because the graph shows a voltage that rises from low to high. The best way to make pulses for the clock input is to build an astable.

Objectives

In this section you will learn:

how to use a 4017 counter IC

how to make a counter reset at the count you want

how to draw the timing diagrams for counter circuits

to understand the use of counters to produce sequences.

Key terms

Rising edge: when a digital signal changes from a low to a high.

links

You learned the term astable in Chapter 7.

A A 0–9 counter

B Digital alarm clock

To make the circuit work the Enable pin and the Reset pin must both be connected to 0 V to make them low. When the Reset pin is high it makes the count go to zero.

If you want to count to less than 9 you can connect the Reset pin to one of the outputs. For example, if you want to count 0,1,2,3,0,1,2,3,0,1… then connect the reset pin to the 4 output so that the counter resets to 0 on the pulse after 3.

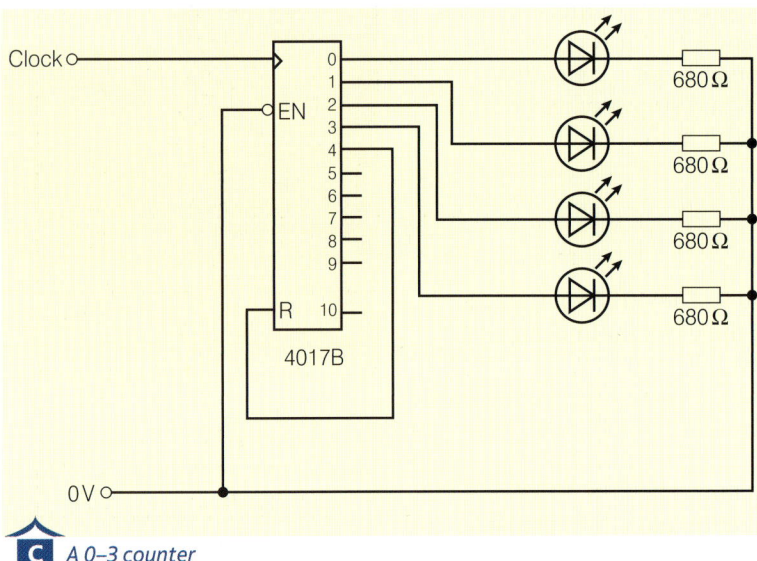

C *A 0–3 counter*

The behaviour of the circuit can be described by a timing diagram which uses graphs to show how the voltages in the circuit change with time. Notice that changes only happen on the rising edge of the clock. Rising edges are shown with an arrow on the clock.

D *A timing diagram, showing how voltage varies with time*

Chapter 8 Latching and counting circuits

Activity

1 Have a go at building the counter circuit in Figure **E**. What happens when you hold the reset button down? Change the circuit so that it only counts from 0–5. Draw the circuit diagram of your solution.

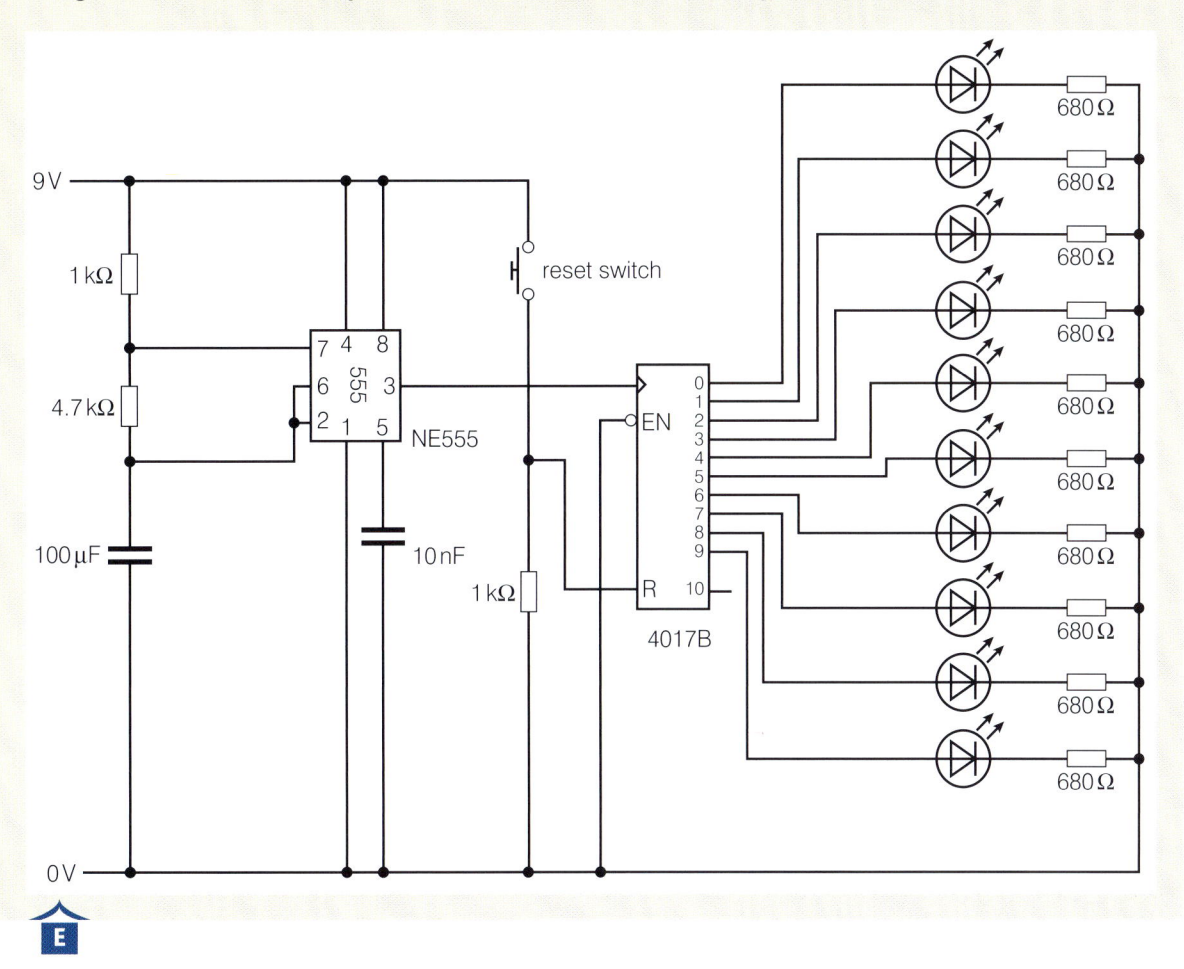

E

Sequences

Lots of electronic systems use sequences where things have to happen in the right order and for the right amount of time. Examples include the functions in a bread-making machine (mixing, resting, baking) or the signals on a set of traffic lights (red, red and amber, green, amber). Counters and logic gates can be used to operate a sequence – the logic turns on each part of the sequence when the counter is on the right number. Here is a system to operate a model of some traffic lights, using red, amber and green LEDs.

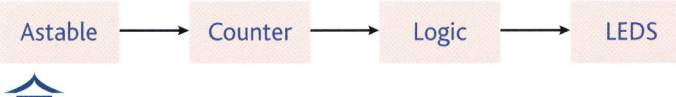

Astable → Counter → Logic → LEDS

F *System diagram for traffic lights*

To produce a sequence it helps to write the sequence next to the numbers in a table.

count	green	amber	red	display
0	0	0	1	red
1	0	1	1	red and amber
2	1	0	0	green
3	0	1	0	amber

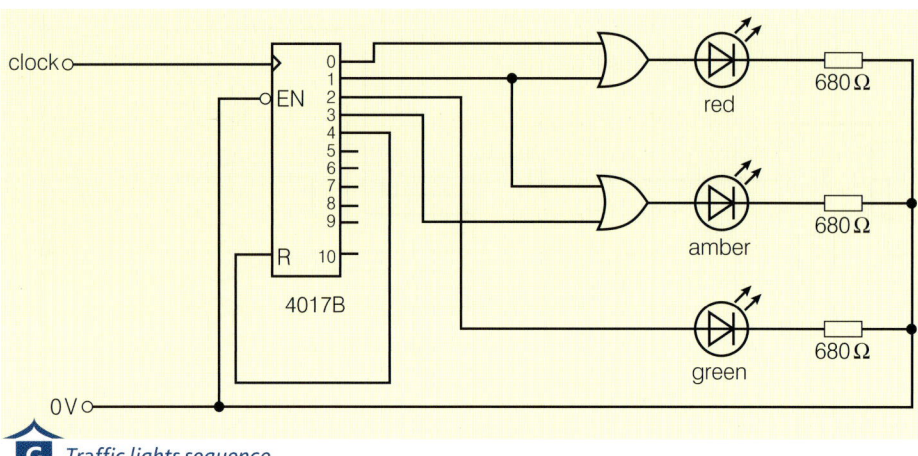

G *Traffic lights sequence*

This means that the red light is on when the count is 0 or 1 so an OR gate is used to connect the red LED to the 0 and 1 outputs.

From the table you can see that amber = 1 OR 3.

Green is only on for 2, so no logic gate is needed just a connection to the 2 output.

The counter needs to reset at 4 because it only needs to count from 0–3.

The sequence above makes all steps of the sequence the same length. To make the green and red lights come on for a longer time than the amber light they need to be on for more than one line in the table.

count	green	amber	red
0	0	0	1
1	0	0	1
2	0	1	1
3	1	0	0
4	1	0	0
5	0	1	0

Activity

2 Have a go at building a traffic light circuit with an astable connected to the clock input. Make sure the circuit works as you expect.

Once you have it working, you could try modifying the circuit to make the red and the green signals longer than the amber and the red and amber.

8.2 Latches and frequency dividers

Data latches

A data latch is a simple electronic memory that just remembers one thing. A data latch can store a 1 or a 0. The **D-type flip-flop** is the electronic component used to make a data latch.

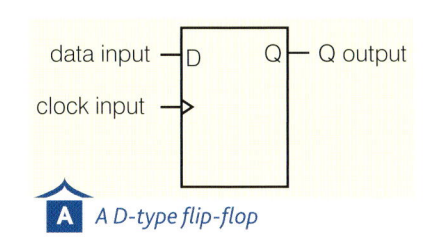

A A D-type flip-flop

Objectives

In this section you will learn:

what a D-type flip-flop does and recognise its symbol

how to draw and interpret the timing diagram for a data latch and know that it is a simple memory

what a frequency divider does and be able to do calculations on frequency divider circuits

how to understand and draw frequency divider circuits and their timing diagrams.

The 'D' in D-type flip-flop stands for data – the digital information that the D-type flip-flop will store. The simplest use of the D-type flip-flop as a latch just uses the clock and data inputs and the output Q. The information at D is copied to Q when the signal at the clock changes from 0 to 1. The change from 0 to 1 is called a rising edge. The behaviour of a D-type flip-flop can be summarised in a timing diagram, as shown in Figure **B**.

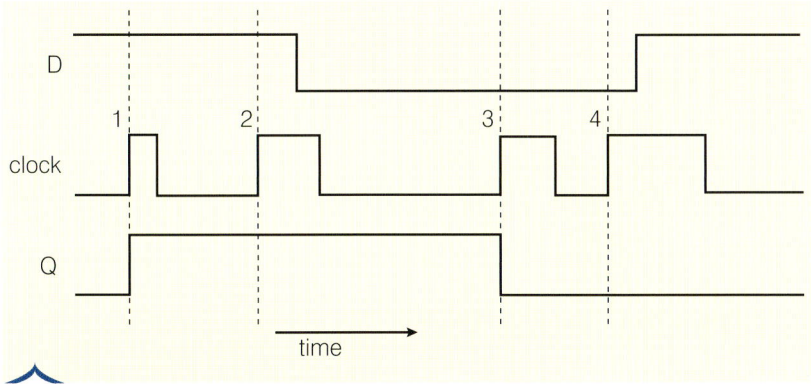

Key terms

D-type flip-flop: an electronic component used to make a data latch.

B Timing diagram for D-type flip-flop

Q only changes on the rising edges of the clock, which are shown by the dotted lines. At rising edge 1, D = 1 so Q becomes 1. At 2, D = 1 so Q stays 1. At 3, D = 0 so Q becomes 0. At 4, D = 0 so Q stays 0.

The inputs for a D-type flip-flop can be produced with switches and the output shown on an LED. This is shown in Figure **C**.

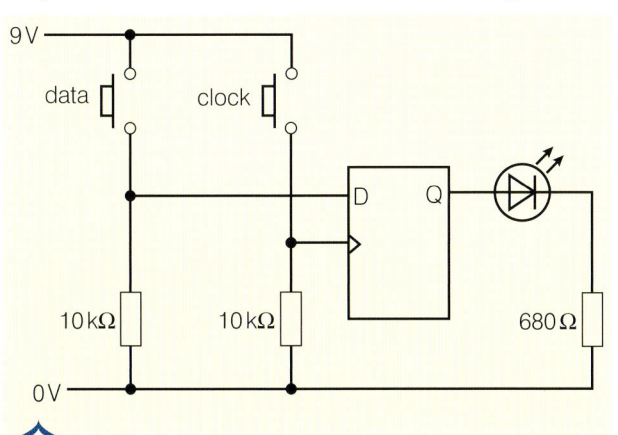

C Inputs and outputs of a D-type flip-flop

To turn the LED on, hold down the data switch to make D high and press the Clock switch to produce a rising edge at the clock. The high is then copied from D to Q and the LED lights up. To turn the LED off make D low by not pressing the data switch and press the Clock switch to produce a rising edge at the clock. The low is then copied from D to Q and the LED turns off.

The D-type flip-flop has two outputs – the Q and $\overline{Q}$ outputs. The line over the Q means NOT, so $\overline{Q}$ means NOT Q. This means that $\overline{Q}$ is always the opposite of Q. When Q = 0 then $\overline{Q}$ = 1 and when Q = 1 then $\overline{Q}$ = 0.

■ Set and Reset

D-type flip-flops also have S and R inputs. The S input is the Set input. When S is high, Q goes high. If you do not need to use S it must be connected to 0V.

The R input is the Reset input. When R is high, Q goes low. If you do not need R it must be connected to 0 V.

Activity

Build the circuit in the figure using a 4013 IC. You must connect the R and S inputs to 0 V. Make sure you can turn the LED on and off using the two switches.

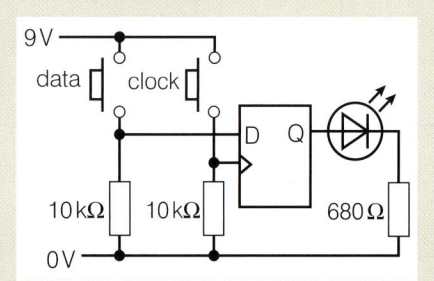

Add another colour of LED with a resistor to the $\overline{Q}$ output and write down what happens in the circuit now.

Note: The 4013 is a dual D-type device, so all the inputs of the second (unused) latch need to be connected to 0V.

D A wristwatch

■ Frequency dividers

Frequency dividers turn a high frequency signal into a low frequency signal. Most watches contain an astable that produces a very accurate 32 768 Hz signal. A watch contains a frequency divider to turn the 32 768 Hz signal into a 1 Hz signal to make the second hand move once a second.

One D-type flip-flop can make a divide-by-2 frequency divider by connecting D to $\overline{Q}$. The input signal goes to the clock input and the output signal comes from the Q output.

Figure **E** shows a divide-by-two circuit. If a 24 Hz signal is put into the divider the output is 24 Hz ÷ 2 = 12 Hz.

E A divide-by-2 circuit

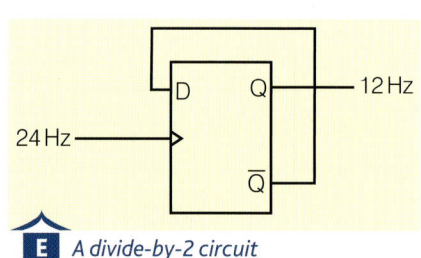

[24 Hz waveform]

[12 Hz waveform]

F *Timing diagram for a divide-by-2 circuit*

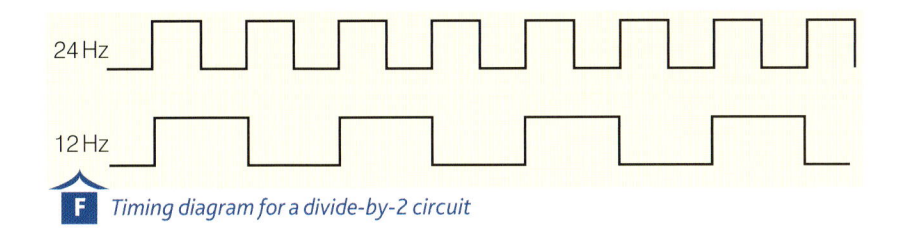

The output changes every time there is a rising edge at the clock input. This works because D is connected to $\overline{Q}$ which makes D the opposite of Q. To divide by more than two we need to use a few divide-by-two circuits.

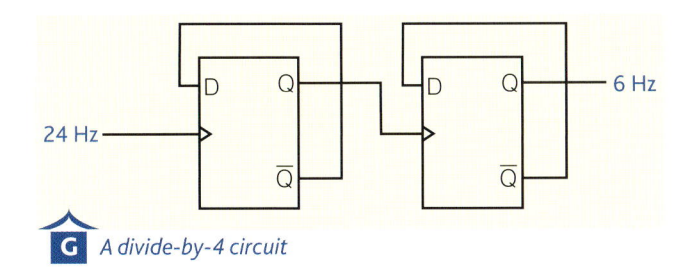

G *A divide-by-4 circuit*

Figure **G** shows a divide-by-four circuit so 24 Hz ÷ 2 ÷ 2 = 6 Hz. Every flip-flop divides by two. To work out how much the circuit divides by, multiply by 2 for each flip-flop so two flip-flops produces $2 \times 2 = 4$. Three flip-flops makes a divide-by-8 circuit: $2 \times 2 \times 2 = 8$.

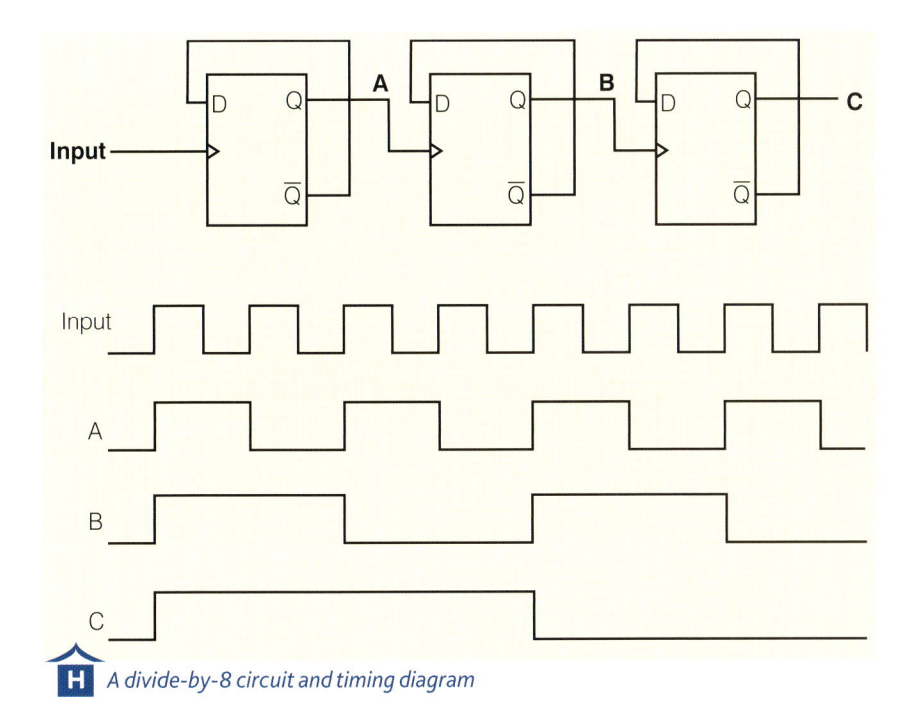

H *A divide-by-8 circuit and timing diagram*

Notice that each line changes at each rising edge of the line above.

To make larger divider circuits just repeat the pattern above by adding divide-by-two circuits, and connect the output of one divide-by-two circuit to the clock of the next divide-by-two circuit.

Summary

Counters change their output every time there is a rising edge at the clock.

Making the reset input high makes the counter output zero.

An output of the counter can be connected to the reset to make the counter reset before 9.

Any sequence can be produced by connecting logic gates to the outputs of a counter.

D-type flip-flops are used for storing digital information. The information at D is stored at Q when there is a rising edge at the clock.

Set makes the Q output high, reset makes Q low.

Connecting $\bar{Q}$ to D makes a D-type flip-flop into a frequency divider.

One divider divides by two; several divider circuits can be used to divide by larger numbers.

Questions

1   **a**   Draw the circuit for a counter to count from 0 to 6.
     b   Draw the timing diagram for your 0 to 6 counter.

2   Complete a table to show the sequence for the circuit in the figure. Describe what happens to the LEDs as the pulses are received by the clock.

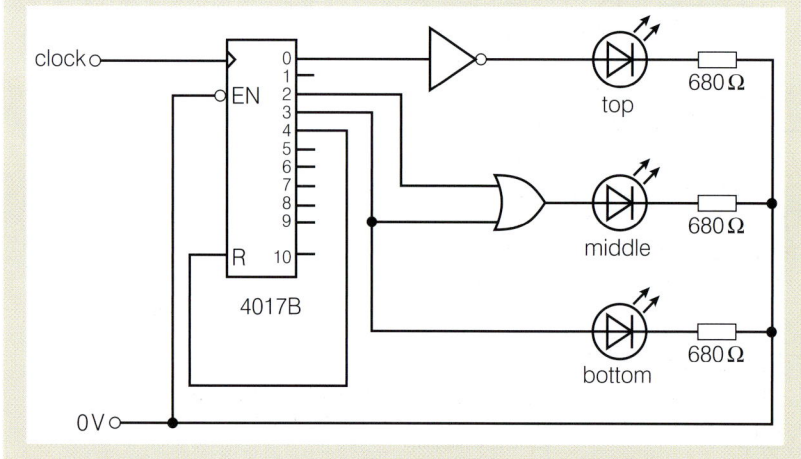

3   Write down two ways to make the output of a D-type flip-flop high.

4   A 96 Hz signal is connected to the input of a divider circuit containing five flip-flops. Draw the circuit and work out the frequency of the output.

5   How many D-type flip-flops are needed to make a divide-by-16 circuit? Draw the timing diagram for a divide-by-16 circuit.

6   How many D-type flip-flops are there in the frequency divider of a watch to turn the 32768 Hz signal into a 1 Hz signal?

9 Comparing signals

9.1 Introducing comparator circuits

The porch light

Suppose that you wanted to build a system which automatically turned on the light in your front door porch when it got dark. Figure **A** shows a possible system diagram, using a light sensor as the input transducer, and a lamp as the output transducer.

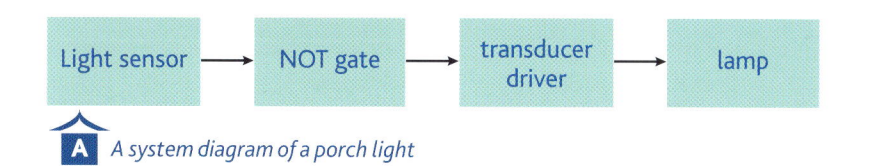

Light sensor → NOT gate → transducer driver → lamp

A A system diagram of a porch light

When it is bright the light sensor in this system produces a high signal. This is fed to the NOT gate, so this produces a low output and the lamp is therefore off. When the light level drops, the signal from the light sensor falls, so the input to the NOT gate goes low. The output of the NOT gate thus goes high and the lamp turns on.

Analogue signals

There are two major problems with this system. They are to do with the type of signal that the light sensor produces. The intensity of daylight can have any value – between zero (in pitch darkness) and some high value in bright sunshine, and all possible levels in between. Any light sensor used will therefore produce a voltage which can change with time between being very small and some high value. Signals that do this are called **analogue signals** (because they are the 'analogue' or copy of the thing being sensed). NOT gates only work with digital signals, and, as you should remember from Chapter 4, these signals are either on or off – nothing in between.

Figure **B** shows the difference between these two types of signal clearly. One is from a microphone – an analogue signal – and the other is the signal from a push-button switch – a digital signal.

The second problem is this. How will we know at what light level the system turns on? There is no way of adjusting this.

Comparing signals

The first problem can be solved by **comparing** the signal from the light sensor with some fixed signal, and when it is bigger than this, generate a digital signal to turn on the lamp. A comparing circuit is needed. Luckily there is a very common, very important and very useful chip that will do just this job.

Objectives

In this section you will learn:

what an analogue signal is and how it differs from a digital signal.

Key terms

Analogue signals: a signal that can have any value between certain set limits.

links

Transducers were introduced in Chapter 2.

links

NOT gates were described in Chapter 4.

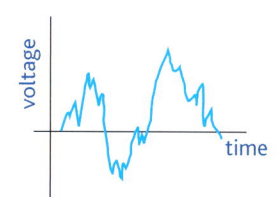

An **analogue** signal from a microphone

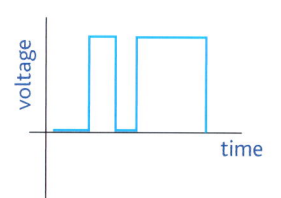

A **digital** signal from a push button switch

B Analogue and digital signals

9.2 The operational amplifier

Just after the Second World War, electronic engineers in America invented a general purpose electronic building block that could be used to amplify signals. They called it the operational amplifier (or the **op-amp**). Transistors – let alone chips – were not even invented then, so it was big and bulky and made using the MOSFET's predecessor – the **thermionic valve**.

Nowadays there are ICs that work as general purpose amplifiers, and there are hundreds of different op-amps on the market. Fortunately, most of them are very similar. Figure **A** shows what a typical op-amp chip looks like, together with the circuit symbol and the names of the pins.

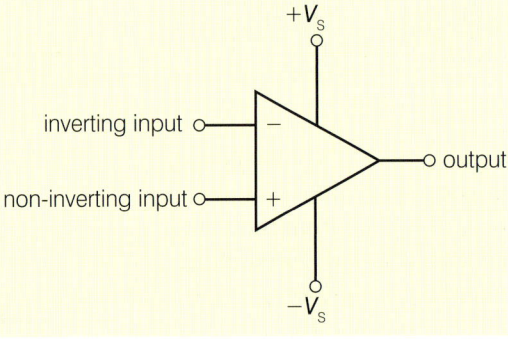

A The op-amp and its pin names

Objectives

In this section you will learn:

to recognise the symbol and connections for the op-amp

to appreciate the limitations in the use and behaviour of the op-amp

what a comparator is, and understand how the op-amp compares signals

the applications of the op-amp comparator.

Key terms

Op-amp: operational amplifier (a general purpose, high gain amplifier chip).

Inverting input: the (−) input of an op-amp.

Non-inverting input: the (+) input of an op-amp.

Saturated: the output of the op-amp is at the + supply or at 0 V.

Ideal op-amp: an op-amp with a gain of infinity (∞).

Gain

The **inverting input** and the **non-inverting input** are where the signal to be amplified is connected, and what the op-amp does is to amplify **the difference between the voltages at these two inputs**.

The **output** is the amplified signal, and the $+V_S$ and $-V_S$ pins are where the power supply is connected.

The amount by which the op-amp amplifies the input signal is called its amplification factor or **gain**.

For most op-amps, gain is enormous – anything between about 50 000 (5×10^4) and 1 000 000 (1×10^6). Most of them are around 100 000 (1×10^5).

links

You will look at amplification and gain in more detail in Chapter 10.

Why so big?

The reason is that since it is a general purpose device, the manufacturers have no way of knowing how much amplification the user needs – so they make it as big as possible. By connecting it with other components the gain can then be made exactly what you want. The huge gain makes the op-amp behave in a very useful way, perfect for our comparing circuit.

AQA Examiner's tip

Although the diagram in Figure **A** shows a positive and negative supply, in this cause you will use positive (+9 V) and zero (0 V) for the op-amp.

Chapter 9 Comparing signals 75

Saturation

In the circuit in Figure **B**, the op-amp has been connected to a 12 V supply, its inverting input has been connected to a 1.5 V cell, and its non-inverting input has been connected to a 9 V battery.

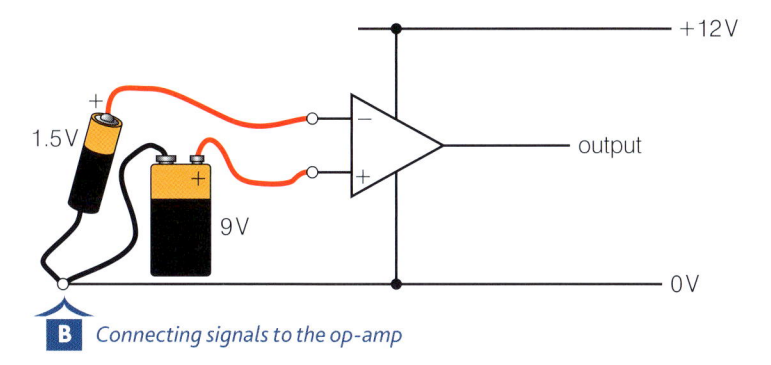

B *Connecting signals to the op-amp*

Remember that it is the *difference* between the voltages at the two inputs which gets amplified. Here, the difference is 7.5 V, so the op-amp amplifies this by 100 000 times to produce the output.

That means that the output voltage will be 7.5 × 100 000 or 750 000 volts! In fact, the op-amp would produce this if it could (and its insides could withstand it), but it only has a supply of 12 V. So what the output does is the best that it can – it goes to +12 V. We say that the op-amp **saturates** at the supply voltage.

Supposing the voltages at the inputs are now swapped, so that 1.5 V goes to the non-inverting input, and 9 V goes to the inverting input. The size of the difference is still 7.5 V, but this time it is the non-inverting input that is the bigger of the two. When this is the case, the op-amp treats the difference as being negative. So its output would want to go to −7.5 × 100 000 or −750 000 V; but it cannot get that low, so it saturates at 0 V.

The enormous gain means that it will behave like this even if the voltages at the op-amp inputs were made very close. Say the input voltages were now 1.5 V and 1.499 V. The difference is 0.001 V, so the output would be 0.001 × 100 000 = 100 V. The op-amp cannot manage this, so it will again saturate at +12 V.

The bigger an op-amp's gain, the smaller the voltage difference needs to be for it to behave like this. We say that the **ideal op-amp** has a **voltage gain of infinity** (∞).

Look at Table **C**. These are examples of what the ideal op-amp would produce for different combinations of input voltages, just to help emphasise what it does. This time it uses a power supply of 9 V. Make sure that you are happy with this before moving on.

C *Op-amp behaviour (power supply 9 V)*

inverting input /V	non-inverting input /V	output
0.5	1.3	9
3.6	3.5	0
7.4	7.398	0
0.015	0.016	9

The op-amp is behaving like a really good 'signal comparer'. Depending upon which input is the bigger voltage, by even a small amount, the output will go to either +12 V or 0 V. This circuit is very useful, and it is called a **comparator**.

The output of the comparator is a digital signal. It can only ever be 0 V or 12 V. The input voltages could have any values we choose – it just depends on what the signals are that we want to compare. So this circuit is actually converting an analogue signal (or signals) into a digital signal. It is a simple but useful example of an **analogue-to-digital converter**, or **ADC**.

Key terms

Comparator: a circuit that compares two signals.

ADC: analogue-to-digital converter. A device which converts an analogue signal to a digital one.

Activity

You can verify the operation of the comparator quite easily. You will need an op-amp, two red LEDs, two yellow LEDs, two 470 V resistors, a 9 V battery and two variable power supplies for the inverting and non-inverting input signals.

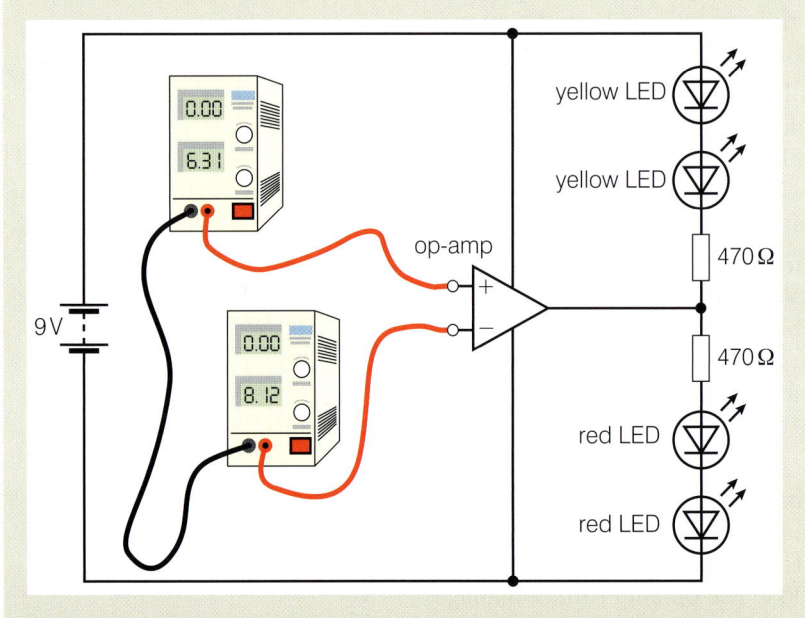

links

There is more about the ADC in Chapter 13.

AQA Examiner's tip

How do you know which op-amp to use if there are so many available? One of the most common types, that has been around since 1968 and was one of the first to be produced commercially in high volumes, is called the 741. For many years this has been the standard in school text books and in examination specifications. Although you can still get it, and it is still usable, the 741 has long been superseded by much better types (much nearer ideal behaviour). For the GCSE any of the following are suitable, and you can get them from many different chip suppliers: TL081, LF351, CA3130, LM301, OP07, MC33201. They are all 8-pin chips, with exactly the same pin connections.

Be sure not to turn up either of the power supplies beyond 9 V – the op-amp will not like it. Now, set the power supplies to different combinations of voltages – you could use the examples from Table 9.1. When the op-amp output is high (9 V), the red LEDs will come on; when it is low (0 V), the yellow LEDS will come on. You can check that the right LEDs come on for the different combinations of input voltages.

Two red (and two yellow) LEDs have been used because not all op-amps are able to saturate at the supply or at 0 V. This means, for example, that when the output is supposed to be 0 V it could actually be as high as 2 V. This would be just enough to turn the red LED on when it was really supposed to be off. With two LEDs the voltage would not be high enough to do this.

9.3 Sensing the light

The comparator will be perfect as the comparing circuit for the porch light. It will compare the signal from the light sensor with a fixed level signal.

The next question to answer is what are we going to use as a light sensor? What we need is something that gives a voltage which gets bigger as the light level increases. A solar cell would do, of course, but they are expensive. There is a much cheaper and very popular alternative to this, and it is called a **light-dependent resistor**, or **LDR** for short. In Figure **A** there is a picture of a few very common LDRs, together with the LDR symbol.

The material from which the LDR is made changes its resistance with light level. Figure **B** shows the shape of the relationship between the resistance and the light level for a typical type of LDR.

You can see that the LDR's resistance gets lower as the light level increases. This is called a **negative coefficient**. The resistance range is very big; in bright daylight the resistance of the LDR could be as low as 500 Ω, and in complete darkness as high as 2 MΩ ($2 \times 10^6 \, \Omega$). One of the most common types is called the NORP12.

> **Objectives**
>
> In this section you will learn:
>
> what an LDR is, its symbol and characteristics, and know how it is used in a comparator circuit.

> **Key terms**
>
> **LDR (Light-dependent resistor):** a sensing device whose resistance changes with light level.

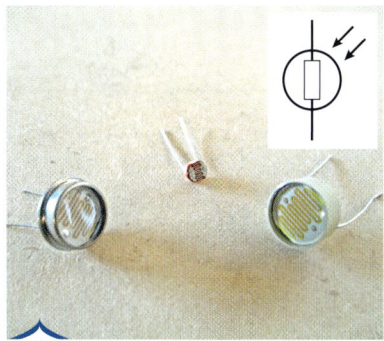

A *The LDR and its circuit symbol*

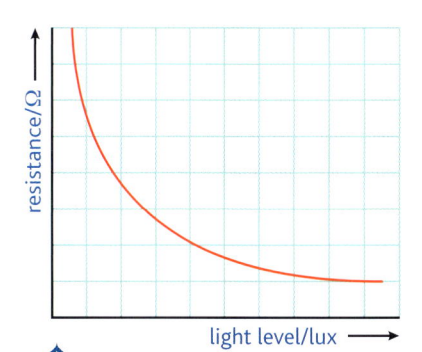

B *The LDR characteristic*

Activity

Seeing the LDR in action is very easy. All you need is a NORP12 LDR, a 9 V battery (or a power supply) and a white LED. The circuit is shown below.

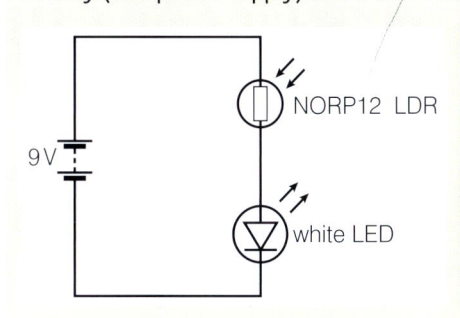

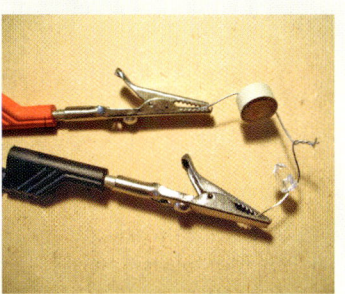

1. Connect the long (+) lead of the LED and one lead of the LDR together. The other (−) lead of the LED then connects to battery − and the other lead of the LDR goes to battery +.

2. Now, turn the LED so that it is pointing towards the LDR, as shown above. This makes the demonstration work a bit better!

3. When you switch on, the LED should light. If you now slowly put your finger or a piece of card in between the LED and the LDR it should get dimmer. If you can manage to cover up the LDR completely, the LED should go out.

4. If you do not have the LED pointing at the LDR, it will still get dimmer as you cover up the LDR – but it does not glow quite as brightly when the LDR is not covered as it did before. Why is this?

9.4 The voltage divider

So, how do we use the LDR in our porch light system? There seems to be a major problem that you may have spotted – the LDR itself does not give out a voltage. The LDR needs to be connected into a circuit which will make use of the LDR's resistance change to give a changing voltage. The circuit we use is called a **voltage divider**, and is shown in Figure **A**.

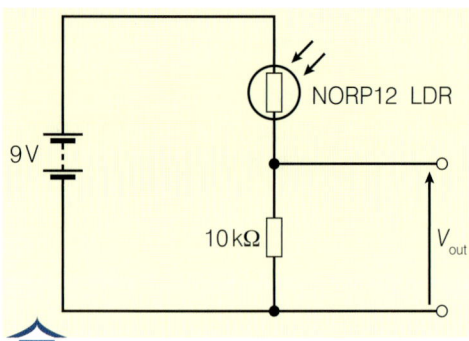

> **Objectives**
> In this section you will learn:
> what a voltage is, and how to use it
> how to calculate the output of a voltage divider.

A *The LDR in a voltage divider circuit*

> **Key terms**
> **Voltage divider:** a circuit which uses two resistors to divide a voltage into two smaller voltages.
> **Variable resistor:** a resistor whose value can be changed or adjusted.

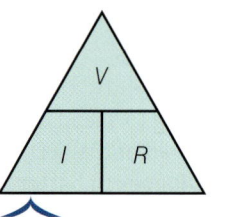

Why is Figure **A** called a voltage divider? V_{out} will be less than 9 V because the battery voltage is *shared* between the two resistances – the 10 kΩ and the LDR. In other words, the battery voltage has been **divided** between the two resistances. It is a very useful circuit, and is frequently used in an electronic system when a voltage smaller than the power supply is needed.

Using Ohm's law

How do we work out the size of V_{out}? Chapter 3 will be useful here. It is a series circuit so Ohm's law can be used to work out the total current, then used again to work out the voltage across the 10 kΩ resistor – which is V_{out}. Let us assume that the LDR has a resistance of 5 000 Ω. The total resistance of the circuit is then 5 000 Ω + 10 000 Ω = 15 000 Ω.

Using Ohm's law:
total current is given by $I = \dfrac{V}{R}$

$$= \dfrac{9}{15\,000} \text{ A}$$

$$= 0.0006 \text{ A (or 0.6 mA)}$$

B *Ohm's law formula triangle*

Because this is a series circuit, the current flows through the resistor as well as the LDR. Ohm's law can be used again to find the voltage across the resistor:

the output, V_{out}, is given by $V = IR$

$$= 0.0006 \times 10\,000 \text{ V}$$

$$= \mathbf{6\,V}$$

The battery voltage of 9 V has been shared between the resistor and the LDR – it has been **divided** between the two. So the resistor must have 9 V − 6 V or 3 V across it (if you do the Ohm's law sums for this you should get 3 V as the answer).

Now, suppose the light level increases. The resistance of the LDR will reduce. If you look at the circuit and the equation, you will see that the current, I, will increase, so V_{out} will increase. We now have a circuit that gives a voltage which increases as the light level increases (and of course reduces as the light level reduces).

Next, the second problem that was discovered with the porch light system in Topic 9.1. How can the voltage be made easily adjustable? (Remember that we need to be able to alter the light level at which the porch light comes on).

If the fixed resistor in the LDR voltage divider is replaced with an 'adjustable' resistor, then the voltage can be changed at a particular light level. A component that does this is called a **variable resistor**.

The voltage divider equation

There is another way to find V_{out}, using the ideas of proportion:

$$V_{out} = 9 \times \frac{R}{(R + R_{LDR})}$$

where R is the value of the resistor, and R_{LDR} is the resistance of the LDR.

So, in the example above:

$$V_{out} = 9 \times \frac{10\,000}{(10\,000 + 5000)}$$

$$= 9 \times \frac{10}{15}$$

$$= 6\,V$$

In a more general form, the equation looks like this:

$$V_{out} = V_{in} \times \frac{R_2}{(R_1 + R_2)}$$

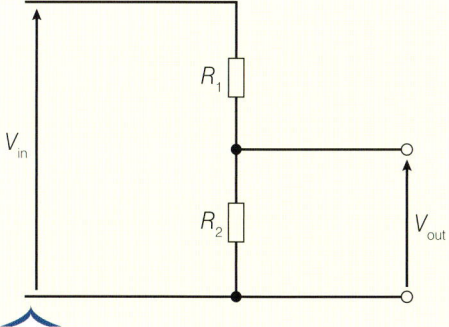

C The general form of the voltage divider

This equation is called the **voltage divider equation** and it can be a much quicker and easier way to find the output voltage than using Ohm's law directly. You can, however, use either method.

9.5 The porch light circuit

Now we have a light sensor and circuit that will give us a voltage that depends on light level, and a comparator to compare this with some fixed signal. How do we produce this fixed signal? The easiest way to do this is with another voltage divider.

If we put all this together, and add a transducer driver for the lamp, we get the circuit shown in Figure **A**.

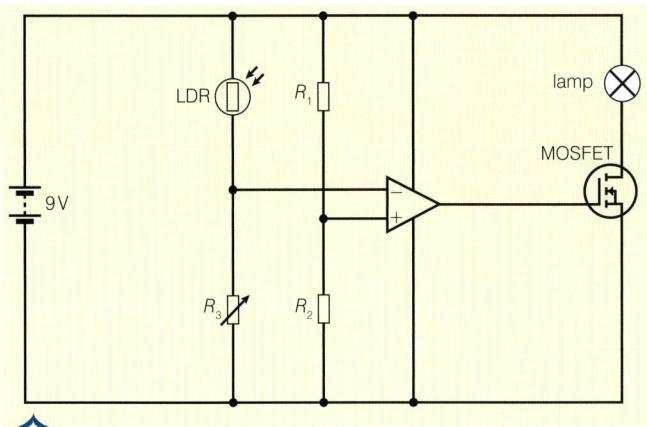

A *The full porch light circuit*

The resistor with an arrow through it, R_3, is the variable resistor, and this is the one that will be adjusted to alter the light level at which the lamp comes on. It is in series with the LDR, forming the voltage divider. The output of this voltage divider is connected to the inverting input of the op-amp, so as the light level changes so the voltage at the inverting input will change. R_1 and R_2 also form a voltage divider, and the output of this is connected to the non-inverting input of the op-amp.

This is how the circuit works. It is easier if the values of R_1 and R_2 are equal. The voltage at the non-inverting input will be half the supply voltage, or 4.5 V (remember – the supply voltage will be shared, and the resistors are equal so it will be shared equally). If it is really light, the resistance of the LDR will be very low, much lower than the value of R_3. The voltage at the inverting input will be much higher than 4.5 V (check the voltage divider equation to make sure you are happy with this). This means that the op-amp output will be 0 V. If it becomes dark the resistance of the LDR rises. At some point, it will equal the value of R_3, and as soon as it goes higher than this, the voltage at the non-inverting input will fall below 4.5 V. The output of the op-amp will then go high, to +9 V, and the lamp will come on.

If R_3 is altered, then the light level at which the resistance of the LDR is equal to R_3 will change.

In other words, R_3 is our light level adjuster.

Activity

Have a go at building the porch light system. You may need to do some calculations to find a suitable value for the variable resistor R_3, but for the other two resistors, 10 kΩ each is a good starting point. Also, make sure that the lamp you use can take 9 V, or else your circuit will work only very briefly!

Objectives

In this section you will learn:

how a comparator circuit works

how to recognise the circuit diagram of an op-amp comparator using voltage dividers

how to perform calculations on an op-amp comparator to determine switching levels.

AQA Examiner's tip

You do have to be able to explain how this type of circuit works. It could be a different arrangement. For example, the LDR and the resistor R_3 may be swapped round. This would create a circuit in which the lamp turns on when the light level gets high. Some questions may show the same voltage dividers as in Figure A, but with the connections to the inputs of the op-amp swapped. This again will produce a different behaviour.

You may also be given a graph of the characteristic of the LDR, and be asked to read off the value of its resistance at a particular light level. Using this information, you may then be asked to work out what the LDR's voltage divider resistor value has to be if the comparator is to switch at this light level.

Be ready for all possible circuit and question variations!

Chapter 9 Comparing signals

9.6 Sensing other things

The circuit in Topic 9.5 can be adapted to sense other things as well. Provided that the sensor we use has a resistance which changes with the quantity it is sensing, then the circuit will work (provided the sensor and the voltage dividers are connected to the correct inputs of the op-amp).

The thermistor

One of the most common applications is to use the circuit to switch something on (or off) at a particular temperature. A heat-dependent resistor can be used. It is called a **thermistor**.

Figure **A** shows a picture of three types of thermistor, and the circuit symbol for a thermistor.

The thermistor behaves in exactly the same way as the LDR – but in response to temperature changes, not light. The range of resistances is similar too. It has what is called a **negative temperature coefficient** or **NTC**, just like the resistance-light characteristic of the LDR. Everything that was done to develop the circuit for the porch light could have been done for, say, a greenhouse temperature alarm. In this case, when the *temperature* fell below a set level, an *alarm* would come on. So there's nothing new to learn (phew) – but it might help to cement all the ideas in this chapter if we use the temperature alarm as an example, and do some working out.

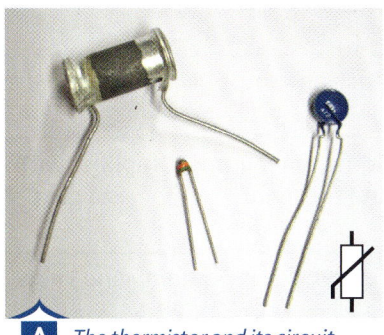

A *The thermistor and its circuit symbol*

Figure **B** shows the full circuit, using a thermistor as the sensor, and alongside is its characteristic curve. The variable resistor sets the temperature at which the alarm sounds, and the power supply is this time 12 V.

Let us suppose that the alarm temperature is to be 5 °C.

What value does the variable resistor have to be set to in order that the alarm buzzer switches on at 5 °C?

First, work out the fixed voltage at the non-inverting input.

Using the voltage divider equation:

$$V_{out} = V_{in} \times \frac{R_2}{(R_1 + R_2)}$$

$$= 12 \times \frac{8.2 \,k\Omega}{3.9 \,k\Omega + 8.2 \,k\Omega}$$

$$= 12 \times \frac{8200}{12\,100}$$

$$= 12 \times 0.68$$

$$= \mathbf{8.16\,V}$$

Objectives
In this section you will learn:

what a thermistor is, its symbol and characteristics, and how it is used in a comparator circuit.

Key terms

Thermistor: a sensing device whose resistance changes with temperature.

Negative temperature coefficient (NTC): a characteristic of the thermistor, where its resistance reduces as the temperature increases.

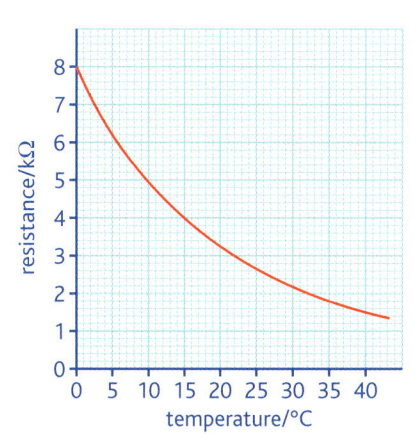

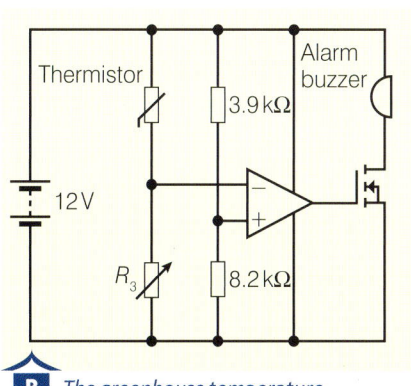

B *The greenhouse temperature alarm circuit*

The comparator will switch when the voltage at the inverting input is just below this. From the graph, the resistance of the thermistor at 5 °C is about 6.2 kΩ. So this value, together with the variable resistor, must produce 8.16 V at the inverting input at the switching point.

We need to use the voltage divider formula again, but this time backwards.

$$V_{out} = V_{in} \times \frac{R_3}{(R_{th} + R_3)}$$

where R_{th} is the resistance of the thermistor.

$$8.16 = 12 \times \frac{R_3}{(6.2\,k\Omega + R_3)}$$

If you rearrange this (have a go), you should get a value for R_3 of $\approx 13\,k\Omega$. So, when the variable resistor is set to this value, the alarm will sound when the temperature drops to 5 °C.

Summary

An analogue signal is one which can have any value between set limits, like the signal from a microphone.

An op-amp (operational amplifier) is a general purpose amplifier with a very high gain – around 100 000 – and the ideal op-amp has a gain of ∞.

You should be able to recognise the symbol for the op-amp and know the five pin names.

The op-amp amplifies the difference in voltage between its inverting and non-inverting inputs.

Saturation is when the output of the op-amp is at the supply voltage or at 0 V.

When the op-amp is connected so that it can be used for comparing voltages it is called a comparator circuit.

An ADC is an analogue-to-digital converter, changing an analogue signal into a digital one.

In the comparator circuit the op-amp is behaving like a simple ADC.

You should be able to recognise the symbol for and understand the behaviour of an LDR and a thermistor.

The resistance of the LDR reduces as the light level increases.

The resistance of the thermistor reduces as the temperature increases.

You should be able to recognise the voltage divider circuit and understand what it does.

You should be able to calculate the voltage from a voltage divider circuit, and recognise the voltage divider formula

$$V_{out} = V_{in} \times \frac{R_2}{(R_1 + R_2)}$$

You should be able to describe the operation of a comparator circuit that uses voltage dividers with either an LDR or a thermistor as the sensor.

AQA Examiner's tip

You are never likely to get a question as complicated as the greenhouse alarm; and you will always be led through the various stages of any calculation – so don't panic! But you do need to understand how to use Ohm's law or the voltage divider formula to work out the voltages at the op-amp inputs.

Thermistors behave exactly like LDRs, so you are just as likely to get a comparator question based on a temperature alarm circuit as you are a light-level circuit. All the theory is exactly the same, and even the graphs are the same shape!

Questions

1 Which of the following are analogue, and which are digital?
a The signal from a light switch.
b The voltage from the pressure sensor in a weighing machine.
c The signal that drives the buzzer in an alarm clock.
d The signal from a pressure mat in a burglar alarm system.
e The mains electricity supply.
f The electrical signal produced by the heart, which is displayed on an ECG monitor.

2 a Draw the circuit symbol for the op-amp, and, by referring to your drawing, explain how this device behaves.
b Using an example, explain what is meant by *saturation*.

3 An op-amp can be used as a comparator.
a Explain how the op-amp comparator works.
b Why can it be thought of as a simple ADC?

4 Give the symbols for an LDR and for a thermistor; explain what each is used for and what their characteristics are.

5 The graph below shows the characteristic curve of one particular type of thermistor.

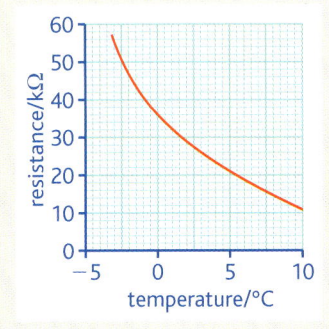

a Using the graph, determine the resistance of the thermistor at:
  i 0 °C
  ii 2 °C
b This thermistor is now connected into a voltage divider circuit, as shown.

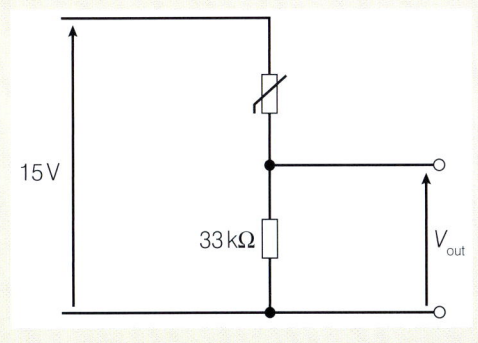

What will be the output voltage, V_{out}, at each of the two temperatures in part **a**?

10 Audio systems

10.1 What is an audio system?

Audio systems are used to process sound signals (e.g. from radio, telephone and TV). The processing will make the signal bigger and may also change its tone. Audio systems often have many inputs and outputs so that the user can listen to sounds from one of many sources, and possibly record them. The inputs can come from a tuner (which receives signals from radio stations), a CD player, a microphone, a DVD player, a computer and an MP3 player. An amplifier subsystem processes the input signals to produce the outputs for the speakers, headphones or recording device. The recording device stores the sound signal on a CD, DVD or memory in an MP3 player.

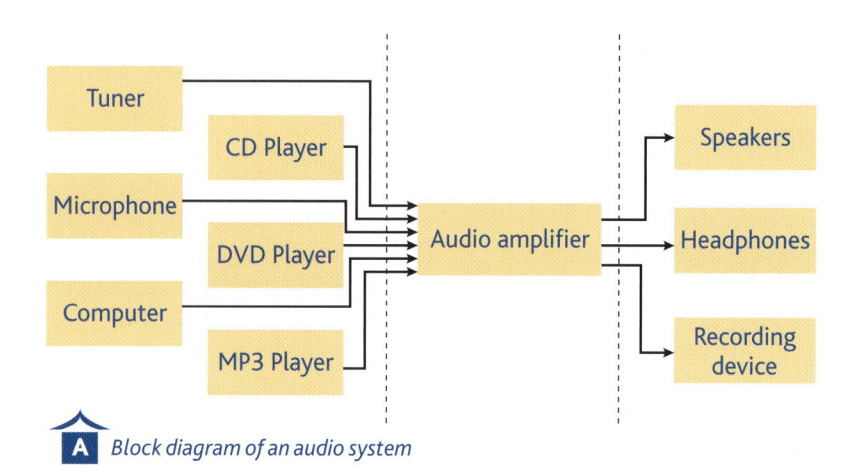

A *Block diagram of an audio system*

Objectives

In this section you will learn:

what an audio system is

to understand the use and operation of audio amplifiers

how to calculate the voltage gain of amplifiers

how to calculate the bandwidth of amplifiers

about electrical noise.

Key terms

Voltage gain: ratio of amplifier output voltage to amplifier input voltage.

links

You learned about loudspeakers in Chapter 7.

Audio amplifiers

You can get the whole circuit for an audio amplifier in an IC. The job of the audio amplifier is to make the input signal bigger, so it can drive, for example, loudspeakers. There are lots of different audio amplifier ICs available. The LM386 (Figure **B**) is common and easy to use.

B *An LM386 IC*

Voltage gain

Audio amplifiers increase the voltage of a signal. The voltage of a signal is **multiplied** by the amplifier.

The number that the input voltage is multiplied by is called the **voltage gain**. We use the symbol G_V for voltage gain. Gain has no units, it is just a number. The equation for voltage gain is

$$G_V = \frac{V_{out}}{V_{in}}$$

where: G_V = voltage gain; V_{in} = input voltage and V_{out} = output voltage.

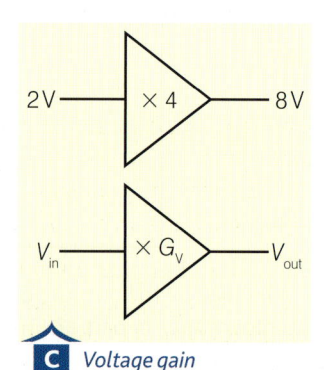

C *Voltage gain*

Activity

1 Build an audio amplifier

Build the circuit shown in Figure **D** on a breadboard. Make sure the circuit works by speaking into the microphone and getting someone else to listen to the loudspeaker. You could make the leads to the loudspeaker very long so you can speak to someone far away.

Test the voltage gain of your amplifier by measuring the input voltage and the output voltage using an ac voltmeter or an oscilloscope.

Extension: Remove the 10 μF capacitor from the circuit. What does this do to the gain?

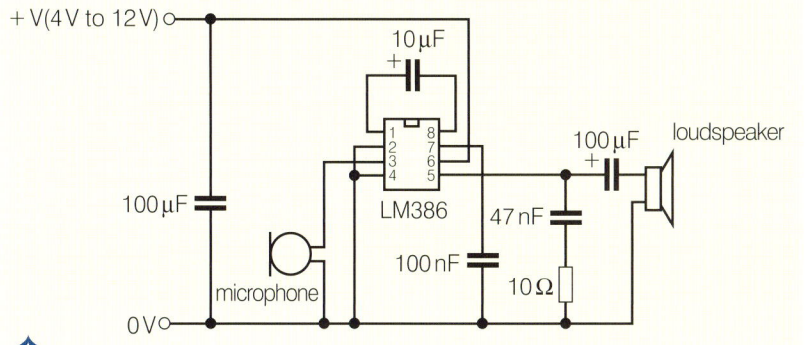

Key terms

Amplitude: the maximum displacement of a wave.

Frequency: the number of complete waves passing through a point each second.

Bandwidth: the range of frequencies where the power gain is at least half the maximum gain.

D *Circuit diagram of the LM386 amplifier*

AQA Examiner's tip

When finding the bandwidth from a graph, draw a pencil line across the graph at half the maximum power to show your working.

Bandwidth

Amplifiers change the **amplitude** of a signal but do not change the **frequency** of a signal. The frequency of the output signal is the same as the frequency of the input signal.

Amplifiers are designed to work with signals of different frequencies. The amplifier will not work well if the frequency of the signal is too high or too low. When the frequency of the signal at the input of an amplifier is too high, the **power gain** is reduced. The relationship between power gain and frequency is usually shown on a graph. Where the power gain is more than half the maximum power gain, the amplifier is working well. The range of frequencies where the gain is at least half the maximum gain is called the **bandwidth**.

The graph shows a maximum power output of 6 W. Half the maximum is 3 W so the bandwidth is 9 kHz − 2 kHz = 7 kHz.

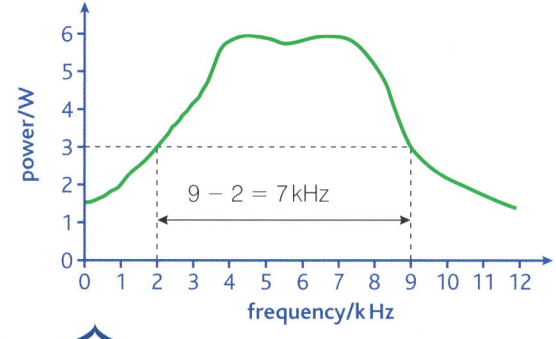

E *Graph of power against frequency*

Noise

Electrical noise is an unwanted signal. Electrical noise can be picked up by the connecting wires in electronic equipment. If electrical noise is picked up on the input wires to an amplifier, the noise will be amplified and can cause problems. Some types of cable pick up more noise than others.

Coaxial cable does not pick up much noise but it is more expensive than ordinary cable. Coaxial cable has a central conductor surrounded by a shield conductor. It is used for connecting microphones and other devices to amplifiers to reduce electrical noise.

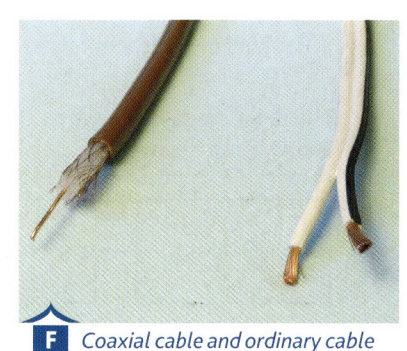

F *Coaxial cable and ordinary cable*

Summary

An audio system processes sound signals to drive e.g. loudspeakers.

Amplifiers are devices that make electrical signals larger.

The input for an amplifier comes from a transducer or circuit that produces an electrical signal from a sound signal.

Voltage gain can be calculated by dividing the output voltage by the input voltage.

Amplifiers do not change the frequency of a signal.

The range of frequencies where the power gain is at least half the maximum gain is called the bandwidth.

Electrical noise is an unwanted signal. It can be reduced by using coaxial cables.

Questions

1 Calculate the missing values in these examples

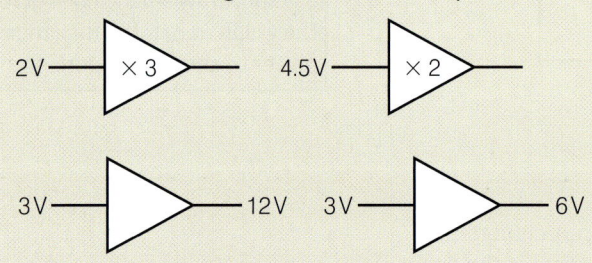

2V — × 3 — ?

4.5V — × 2 — ?

3V — ▷ — 12V

3V — ▷ — 6V

2 The frequency response of an amplifier is shown on the graph below.
a What is the maximum power?
b What is the bandwidth of the amplifier?

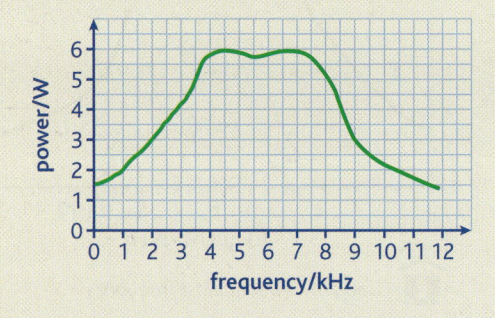

3 What kind of cable would you use to connect an MP3 player to some amplified speakers?

4 The block diagram shows a CD player system. Where is the most important place to use coaxial cable? Explain your answer.

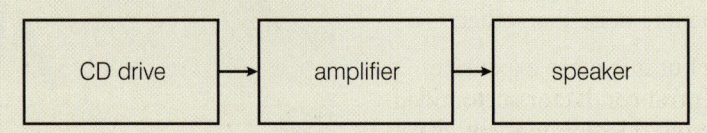

CD drive → amplifier → speaker

11 Power supplies

11.1 What is mains ac?

The electricity available from the mains socket is **ac** but has the same basic property as that found in a circuit powered by a **dc** battery. Both depend upon the fact that electrical charges are made to move in the wires by applying a voltage which gives the charges energy to move.

The main differences between mains voltage and a battery voltage are given in Table **A**.

A *Differences between mains voltage and battery voltage*

property/voltage	mains	battery
voltage value	230 volts (rms)	typical fixed values 1.5 V; 9 V; 12 V
direction	alternating (changes size and direction with a frequency of 50 Hz.)	direct (single direction)
time trace	sinusoidal waveform (current or voltage vs time)	constant positive value (current or voltage vs time)

Objectives

In this section you will learn:

- about the nature of ac mains
- the terms peak value and root mean square.

Labelling the value of the voltage from a battery is relatively easy since it remains steady and sends the current around the circuit in one direction only: e.g. 9 volts dc (the +ve and −ve terminals having a fixed position).

Labelling the mains voltage is more difficult as it is constantly changing in value and direction!

There are two important values associated with an ac supply.

- The **peak value** – this is measured from the mid point of the wave to a peak or trough. The size of the peak allows it to be compared with other supplies. However, the peak only lasts for a split second and is therefore not representative of the whole supply.
- **Root mean square (rms)** – this is based upon the steady dc value that would deliver the same power as the ac. This is the value used to label the mains. So the mains voltage should be labelled 230 volts rms.

The peak voltage and rms voltage are shown in Figure **B** and are related by the following formula.

$$V_{peak} = V_{rms} \times 1.4$$

This means that if the mains voltage is 230 V (rms), the voltage will actually peak at a value of ∼325 V in both the positive and negative directions.

Key terms

ac: alternating current – made to constantly change value and direction by the applied alternating voltage.

dc: direct current – made to flow with a constant value in a fixed direction by an applied fixed value voltage.

Peak value: the maximum positive or maximum negative value that an ac supply achieves.

Root mean square (rms): the equivalent steady value that would provide the same power as the ac supply.

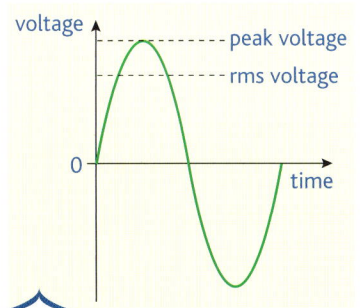

B *An ac time trace showing the peak and rms values*

11.2 Why do we need to convert to dc?

The mains network is a convenient way of bringing electrical power into the home and industry. The voltage stays around 230 V rms and the maximum current a domestic socket can safely deliver is 13 amps.

However, electronic circuits usually contain IC's which are designed to run from fixed low voltage, typically in the range 3 V – 15 V dc.

IC's, which form the backbone of many of the processing subsystems, would fail if the voltages were too high or constantly changed polarity. For this reason we require fixed value, low voltage and single direction supplies to power our electronic circuits.

How can high voltage ac be changed to low voltage dc?

To condition the mains voltage so that it becomes a low voltage dc supply, it must go through a series of clearly defined stages. The conditioning can take place in an external block that plugs into the mains socket (Figure **A**).

However, in some appliances this conditioning takes place on the main circuit board alongside the low voltage dc electronics.

One way of achieving the conversion to a dc supply is to pass the mains voltage through a series of well defined subsystems as shown in Figure **B**.

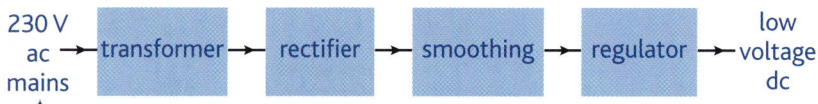

230 V ac mains → transformer → rectifier → smoothing → regulator → low voltage dc

B A block diagram of a regulated power supply system

The transformer

The **transformer** in Figure **C** can clearly be seen to contain two independent coils of wire and an iron core. The circuit symbol in Figure **D** represents the two coils (primary coil and secondary coil) and the iron core. Alternating currents flowing in one coil generate an alternating magnetic field that is enhanced by the iron core. A voltage is then induced in the secondary coil by the moving field.

In a power supply suitable for supplying power to an electronic circuit, we want the output voltage (from the secondary coil) to be smaller than the input voltage (applied to the primary coil). This can be arranged by having fewer turns of wire on the secondary coil than on the primary coil. The step-down voltage ratio can be controlled quite accurately in this way. The output from the transformer is now a low voltage ac supply.

Rectifier

This stage is designed to take the low voltage ac from the transformer and remove the negative part of the cycle. Silicon diodes which have

Objectives

In this section you will learn:

- to understand the need to convert from ac mains to low voltage dc
- about the basic block diagram for the power supply
- how diodes can be used to condition an ac voltage
- to understand the part played by capacitors in power supplies.

A External ac–dc power supply adaptor

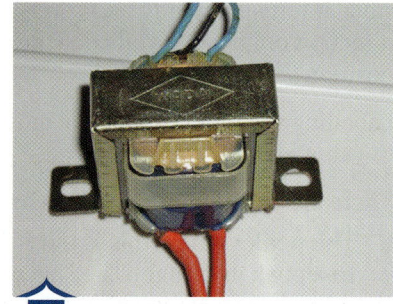

C An electrical transformer

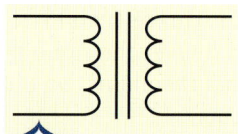

D Transformer circuit symbol

AQA Examiner's tip

It is worth learning the full systems diagram for a regulated power supply.

Chapter 11 Power supplies

a forward voltage drop of about 0.7 V when conducting are used to either block the negative half of the ac cycle completely or reroute it. This can be done using either a **half-wave rectifier** circuit or a **full-wave rectifier** circuit as shown below.

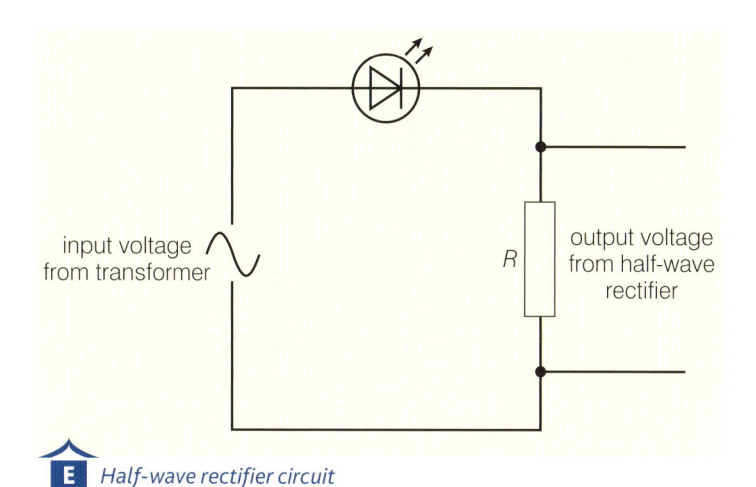

> **Key terms**
>
> **Transformer:** a device used to change the value of an ac supply. It can be used to step the voltage up or down.
>
> **Half-wave rectifier:** a circuit containing a diode used to block out the negative half of the ac cycle.
>
> **Full-wave rectifier:** a circuit containing a number of diodes (diode bridge) used to make both halves of the ac cycle become positive.

E Half-wave rectifier circuit

The advantage of this circuit is that it only uses a single diode to perform the conditioning and as such is a very simple circuit to construct.

The disadvantages of the circuit are:
- Only one half of the power from the full wave is now available for use.
- The output voltage is very lumpy and still not suitable for powering modern electronic circuits.

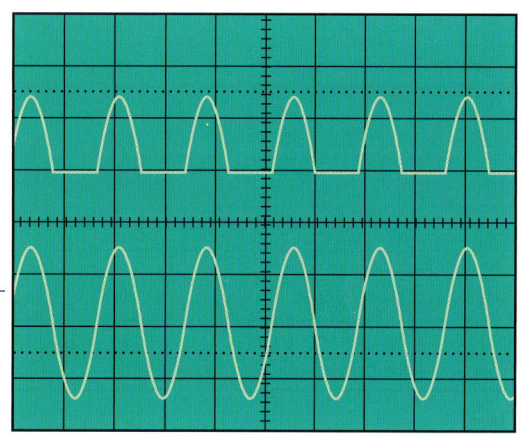

F CRO output and input trace

Activity

1 Building the half-wave rectifier circuit in Figure E

The half-wave rectifier experiment can be carried out safely if the low voltage ac is taken from a laboratory power supply set to 12 V ac. The mains will already have been transformed down inside the power pack. The diode used is an 1N4001 and the load resistor on the output can be 1 kΩ. If a double beam CRO is available then by probing the input to the rectifier from the power pack and the output across the load resistor, the traces as shown in Figure F should be seen.

The full-wave rectifier circuit

It would be much better if we could make use of the available power in both the positive and negative parts of the low value alternating voltage. This can be achieved by using a diode bridge rectifier circuit, as shown in Figure **G**.

> **AQA Examiner's tip**
>
> Learn how to position and draw the four diodes to make a full-wave rectifier.

G *Full-wave diode bridge rectifier*

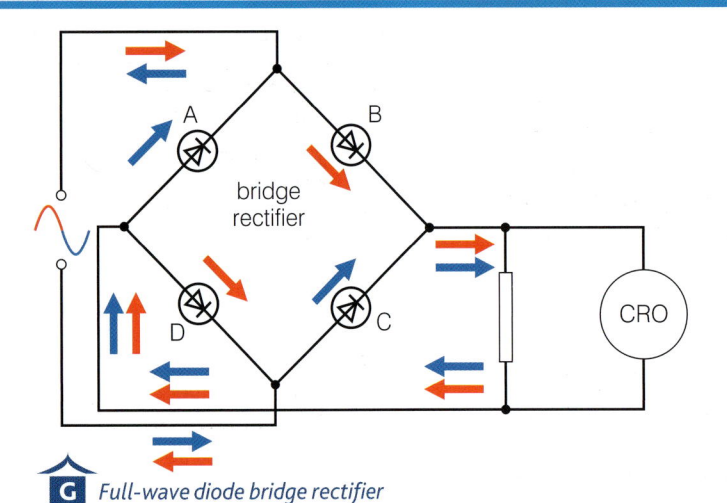

In the circuit in Figure **F**, it does not matter which part of the cycle is present, the current is always made to flow the same way through the load resistor. This leads to the output shown in the bottom trace in Figure **H**.

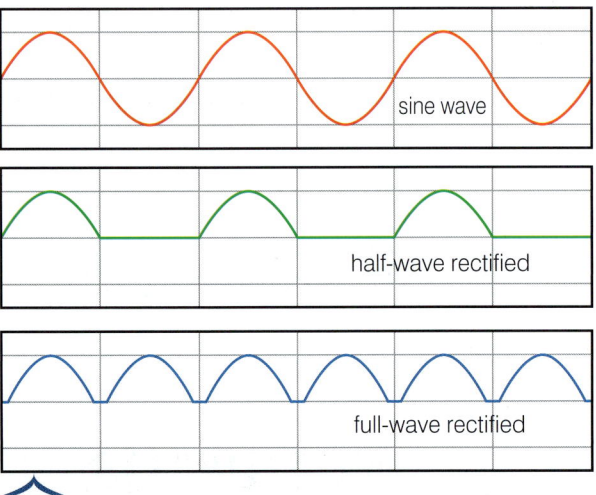

H *Output trace from a full-wave rectifier circuit*

The voltage is now always positive (both parts of the original ac wave are being used) and the size has been reduced by the transformer. However, the output from the full-wave rectifier is still too lumpy to be used by an electronic circuit.

Activity

2 Building the full-wave rectifier

The low voltage input to this circuit is again taken from the output of a laboratory power pack set to 12 V ac.

The diode bridge can either be made up from four 1N4001 diodes (positioned with the correct polarity) or you could use one of the many four-pin packaged bridge rectifiers such as the W005M in a rounded plastic package. The ac input legs and the rectified output legs are clearly marked on the package.

A CRO can be used to probe the input to the bridge rectifier, and the output across a 1 kΩ load resistor should give similar results to those shown in Figure **I**.

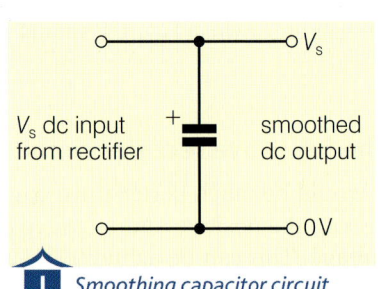

I *Smoothing capacitor circuit*

Chapter 11 Power supplies 91

The smoothing capacitor

The **smoothing capacitor** acts as a reservoir that fills and empties in such a way as to smooth the varying voltage. At this stage, the voltage has almost been turned into a steady dc value, but may still contain some ripple (minor regular variation). The smoothing capacitor circuit is shown in Figure **I** and the effect of the smoothing capacitor on the rectified wave in Figure **J**.

■ The regulator

The dc voltage, as well as still containing some ripple voltage, will be susceptible to loading when in use. As more current is demanded from the supply, the voltage will reduce and needs to be held steady. This is done most easily by the use of a dc regulator IC. This component itself will use some voltage and although the final output voltage will now be fixed, it will be lower than the voltage supplied to it. For example, a 9 V output regulator may well need about 12 V (unregulated) supplied to it. The appropriate dc regulator must be selected based upon the fixed output voltage required. The 78XX series is a popular series of such regulators and is shown in Figures **K** and **L**.

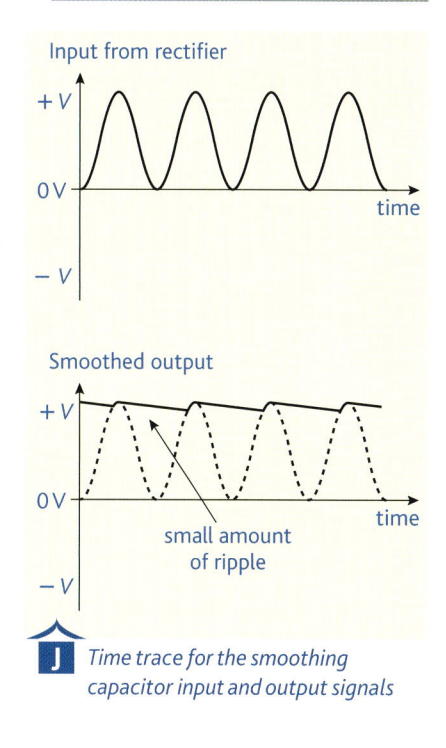

> **Key terms**
>
> **Smoothing capacitor:** a large-value capacitor used as a storage reservoir that acts to reduce the fluctuation (ripple) of the rectified signal.

J Time trace for the smoothing capacitor input and output signals

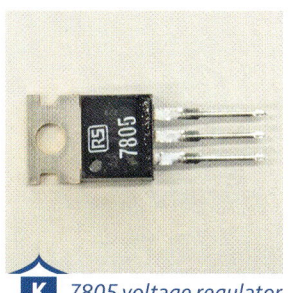

K 7805 voltage regulator with heat sink

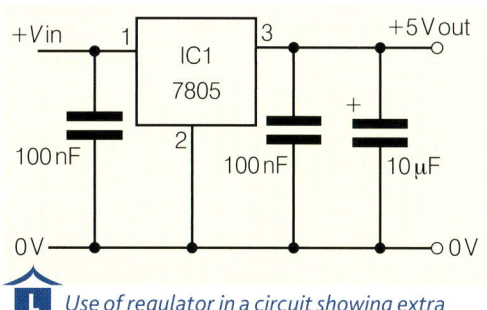

L Use of regulator in a circuit showing extra decoupling capacitors

The final basic low voltage power supply circuit now looks like the one in Figure **M**, which shows all the stages for the low voltage dc power supply.

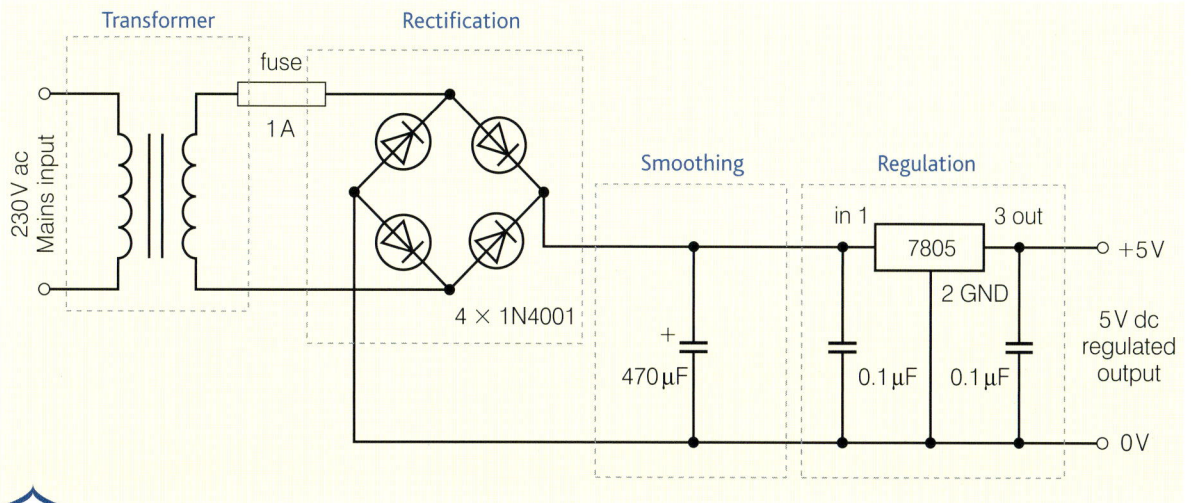

> **AQA Examiner's tip**
>
> You will not need to recall the details of the regulator.

M The basic power supply circuit

Activity

3 Building the full basic power supply shown in Figure M

You can now add to the circuit built in Activity 2 by putting in a 470 µF 63 V electrolytic smoothing capacitor. Place a 1 kΩ load resistor across the capacitor.

Change the value of the smoothing capacitor to see the effect on the ripple voltage but make sure that any capacitor used has at least a 50 V maximum working voltage (MWV).

Change the value of the load resistor to draw more or less current to see the effect on the output voltage. (Make sure that the lower value resistors have higher power ratings to cope with any heat generated and keep well below the maximum current rating for the breadboard (1 A).

Remove the load resistor and add the 7805 regulator (don't forget the extra 0.1 µF polyester capacitors used on the input/output pins of the regulator). Replace the load resistor so that it is now on the output of the regulator. Check that the output is now 5 V.

Summary

Mains voltage varies in amplitude and direction over time.

Mains voltage is labelled using the root mean square value which is related to its peak value.

Electronics circuits require low voltage dc supplies in order to operate.

High voltage ac can be changed into low voltage dc by passing the supply through a:
- step down transformer
- rectifier
- smoothing capacitor
- regulator.

A transformer is a device used to step up or step down the voltage of an ac supply.

Questions

1. The insulation around mains cabling must have a breakdown voltage in excess of the 230 V mains rating. Explain why this must be the case.

2. A laboratory power supply produces a 12 V(rms) output.
   What would you expect the voltage to peak at?
   Why would it be unwise to apply this supply to a circuit containing a capacitor that has a MWV of 16 V?

3. The peak value of an ac supply is measured as 8.4 V on a CRO. What is the best peak value you could expect to see if it had been rectified by:
   a. a half-wave rectifier (single diode)?
   b. a full-wave diode bridge rectifier?

4. Give two reasons why using a half-wave rectifier circuit is usually unsatisfactory for producing the supply for an electronic circuit.

5. A half-wave rectifier has been known to be used as a circuit in a two-position dimmer switch to control the brightness of a filament reading lamp. Explain briefly how this would work.

12 Radio systems

12.1 Radio communication

Audio frequency signal

When we speak or play a musical instrument, the information is produced as an **analogue signal**. These **audio frequency** (AF) sound waves travel at about 330 m/s in air and typically cover a frequency range of between 20 Hz and 20 kHz, which is the accepted frequency range for human hearing.

However, even if we shout, it is unlikely that any useful information will be detected more than 100 m away, as the sound waves quickly lose energy as they travel through air. With the development of radio systems, effective long range communication became available for both social and business needs and sparked the development of the globally connected society.

Radio frequency signal

Rather than being restricted by the inefficiencies of AF sound waves, the electromagnetic spectrum offers us a wide range of waves all travelling at the speed of light (3×10^8 m/s). One part of the spectrum that has been developed specifically for communications is the **radio frequency** (RF). Such waves can travel through the vacuum of space and the energy loss as they travel through air is much less than that of sound.

Unfortunately, in its pure state, the radio frequency portion of the electromagnetic spectrum contains no information of the type needed for communication. The challenge therefore was how to send high quality AF at speed and across distances only achievable by RF. Could the two be combined?

Combining AF and RF

Radio communication really became useful when it was realised that the very fast, go-anywhere radio wave could be used as a **carrier wave** for the information-packed audio wave. Combining the two waves was achieved by the process of **modulation**.

Amplitude modulation

Amplitude modulation, or AM, is achieved by changing (or modulating) the size (amplitude) of the RF wave so that the change mimics the AF information as shown in Figure **A**. AM radio makes use of the medium frequency RF range and provides a relatively cheap and uncomplicated means of mass communication.

The RF is at a much higher frequency than the AF and the resultant wave to be transmitted is gained by combining the two.

> **Objectives**
>
> In this section you will learn:
>
> to understand the basic communication challenge
>
> how modulation can represent signals.

> **Key terms**
>
> **Analogue signal:** a signal that can take up voltage values over a continuous range.
>
> **Audio frequency:** the wave frequency that is associated with sound and lying in the range 20 Hz to 20 kHz.
>
> **Radio frequency:** that part of the electromagnetic spectrum used for radio communication.
>
> **Radio communication:** the means by which information is sent over a distance using radio waves.
>
> **Carrier wave:** the radio wave used to transport the information.
>
> **Modulation:** the act of changing a property of the carrier wave to encode the information on to it.
>
> **Amplitude modulation:** the act of changing the size of the wave to encode the information.
>
> **Frequency modulation:** the act of changing the number of waves produced per second to encode the information.

Signal to be modulated, e.g. speech or music

Carrier radio signal of higher frequency

Carrier wave amplitude modulated by speech or music information

Time

A *Radio wave being modulated by changing its amplitude to mimic the audio information - an example of amplitude modulation (AM)*

AQA Examiner's tip
In an examination question you may be asked to draw the AM and FM resultant waves. Guide / reference lines are usually given, but you should practise drawing the resultant and understand how they combine. For AM – keep the frequency of the RF constant and vary the height of the wave. For FM – draw dotted guide lines across the top and bottom of the RF wave to remind you to keep the size (amplitude) constant. Now change the wave spacing so that the frequency changes.

■ Frequency modulation

Frequency modulation, or FM, is a more complex option and is used more by local radio stations and national stereo transmissions. Here, the frequency of the RF carrier is changed to mimic the AF information as shown in Figure **B**.

Signal to be modulated, e.g. speech or music

Carrier radio signal of higher frequency

Frequency modulated wave

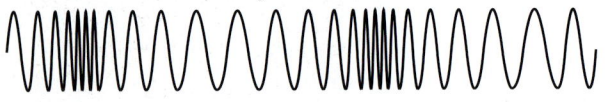

Time

B *Radio wave being modulated by changing its frequency to mimic the audio information - an example of frequency modulation (FM)*

AQA Examiner's tip
In order to gain full credit in an exam question, you must make sure that the original waves and the combined wave patterns match up (see Figures **A** and **B**).

12.2 A simple radio receiver

The aerial

A radio receiving **aerial** is a length of wire used as a **transducer**. This turns the electromagnetic radiation sent out by the radio transmitter into electrical energy. The electromagnetic waves influence the electrons in the metal wire of the aerial and these electrons then move to create a current in time with the frequency of the incoming RF wave. The symbol for the aerial is shown in Figure **B** whilst a more compact form is shown in Figure **C**.

Once the signal is received via the aerial, we need a simple system to detect the information coming in. The system diagram in Figure **A** shows the main stages needed. Each stage plays its own part in getting the information to the listener. The following gives some detail about the science used in each individual subsystem. It should then be possible to identify these different sections in a full circuit.

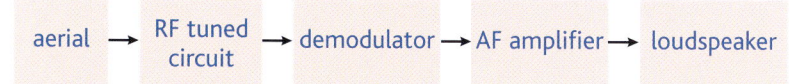

aerial → RF tuned circuit → demodulator → AF amplifier → loudspeaker

A *Systems diagram for a simple AM radio receiver*

The RF tuned circuit

In an **RF tuned circuit**, current can be made to oscillate around the circuit, as energy is interchanged between the electrical field of the capacitor and the magnetic field of the coil (Figure **D**). The oscillations are set up in a similar way to the mechanical oscillations found in a pendulum or swing. For particular values of the components, the energy coming in from just one of the many different radio waves is just at the right frequency to stimulate the circuit. If you change the value of one of the components by using the tuning dial, then the stimulating energy must come from a different radio station, which is broadcasting on a different frequency. In this way you can tune the circuit to respond to the station you want to listen to.

The demodulator

The **demodulator** circuit is responsible for stripping away the RF wave that has carried the information to the receiver, so that just the required AF signal is left. This is done in two stages as shown in Figure **E**:

1. The diode strips away a half of the RF wave but retains the AF.
2. The capacitor acts as a short circuit route for the high frequency RF which then leaves the AF on its own.

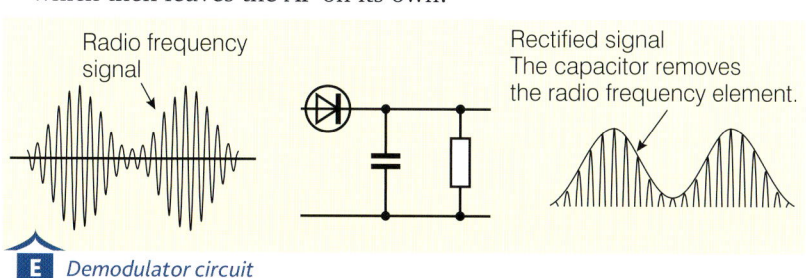

E *Demodulator circuit*

> **Objectives**
>
> In this section you will learn:
>
> to understand the part played by each subsystem in a simple radio receiver
>
> how to explain the terms sensitivity and selectivity.

> **Key terms**
>
> **Aerial:** a wire used to change electrical energy into electromagnetic waves if transmitting, or vice versa if receiving.
>
> **Transducer:** a component that changes energy from one form to another.
>
> **Demodulator:** strips away the RF to leave just the AF.

B *Aerial symbol*

C *More compact form of aerial which then becomes a part of the tuning circuit*

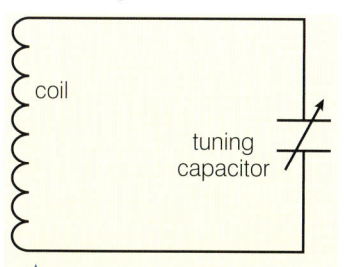

D *RF tuned circuit*

The AF amplifier

The **amplifier** circuit must now boost the AF signal so that it can be used to drive a loudspeaker. This stage may also contain a potential divider circuit which can be used as a volume control. The general symbol in Figure **F** shows how an amplifier subsystem is represented. Sometimes you might find a ×20 or other similar multiplication factor written inside the triangle shape.

The loudspeaker

The loudspeaker is needed so that you can hear the final AF signal. The loudspeaker acts as a transducer turning electrical energy into sound energy (Figure **G**). The signal from the demodulator alone will not usually have enough power to move the cone in the speaker, which is why an amplifier stage is used before it. When looking at a full circuit diagram, the individual subsystems are now easier to identify in Figure **H**.

> **AQA Examiner's tip**
>
> You do not need to know the details of the RF tuned circuit or the demodulator for your GCSE Electronics exam.

links

Amplifiers were covered in Chapter 10.

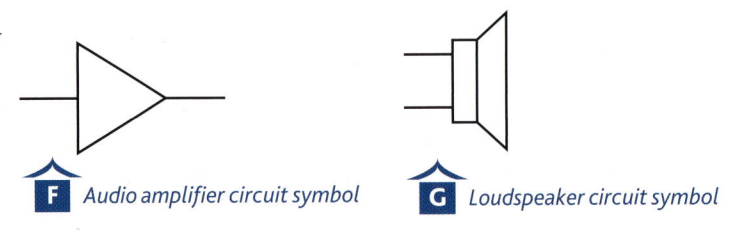

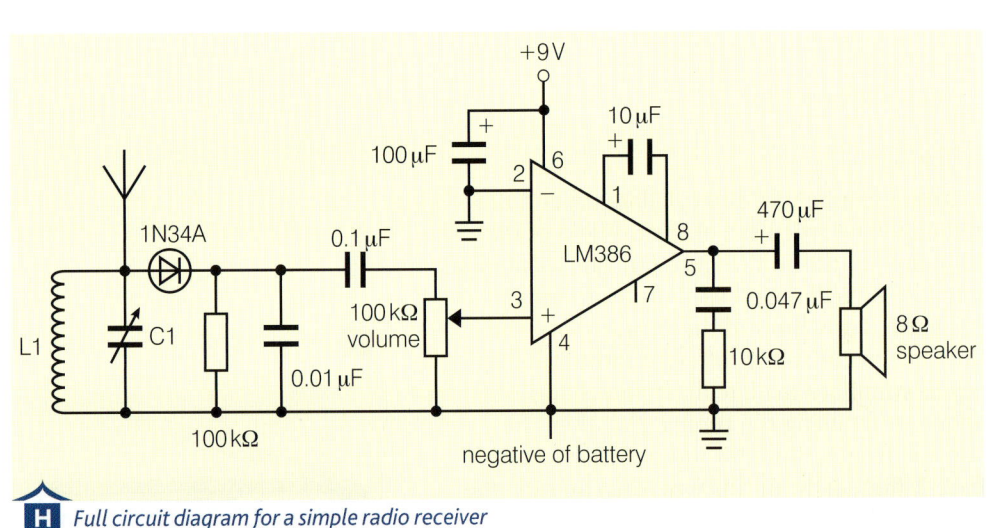

F Audio amplifier circuit symbol

G Loudspeaker circuit symbol

H Full circuit diagram for a simple radio receiver

Sensitivity and selectivity

Two terms that define the quality of a radio receiver are its **sensitivity** and **selectivity**.

- **Sensitivity**: This describes the ability of the receiver to pick up weak signals. The radio signals are often only a few millivolts in strength when they enter the circuit. One way of improving the specification is to add further amplification at the front end of the receiver. An RF amplifier is often to be found between the aerial and the tuner to help boost the signal.
- **Selectivity**: This describes the ability of the receiver to distinguish between two stations that are very close together. In very simple receivers selectivity can be poor. Some improvement in this specification can be achieved by the use of filters. Other more complex circuits are also used to achieve better selection, such as in the superheterodyne receiver.

> **Key terms**
>
> **Sensitivity:** the ability of a radio receiver to receive a weak signal from a distant station.
>
> **Selectivity:** the ability of a radio receiver to distinguish between two radio stations that transmit on frequencies that are close together.

Chapter 12 Radio systems 97

12.3 AM and FM transmissions

Historically, AM was developed before FM. Since FM carries more detailed information than AM, it occupies the higher frequency end of the radio spectrum (see Figure **A**).

> **Objectives**
> In this section you will learn:
> the general properties of AM and FM transmission.

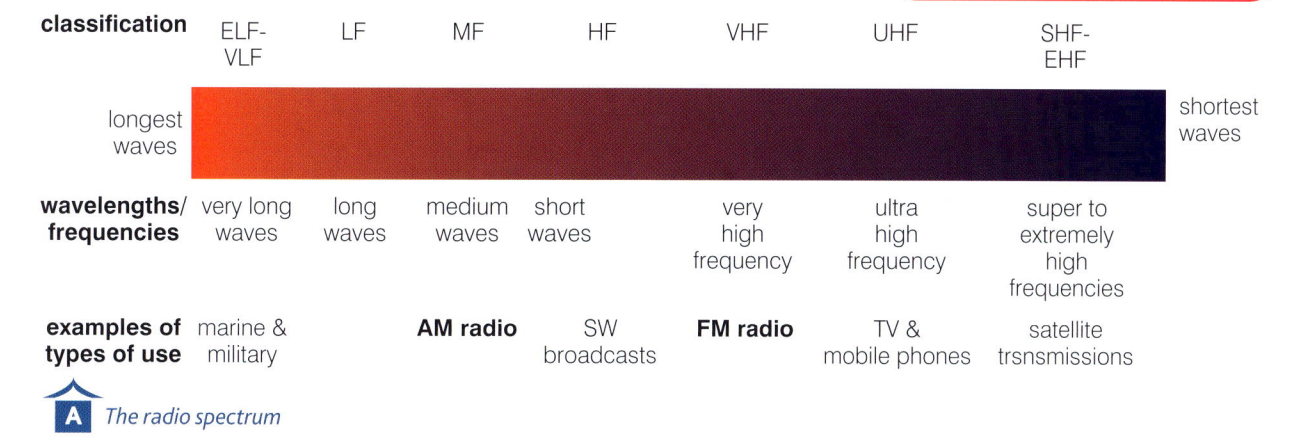

classification	ELF-VLF	LF	MF	HF	VHF	UHF	SHF-EHF
wavelengths/ frequencies	very long waves	long waves	medium waves	short waves	very high frequency	ultra high frequency	super to extremely high frequencies
examples of types of use	marine & military		**AM radio**	SW broadcasts	**FM radio**	TV & mobile phones	satellite trsnsmissions

longest waves — shortest waves

A The radio spectrum

General properties of AM and FM transmissions

AM transmission

The main features of AM transmission are:
- Medium wave (typically 0.3–3 MHz).
- Simple circuitry for relatively cheap communication system.
- Used for national sport, chat and popular music.
- Subject to noise – electrical interference.
- Due to its use in the lower frequency end of the spectrum, there is some sky reflection, leading to wider coverage, but it also leaves it open to atmospheric effects, e.g. fading.

FM transmission

The main features of FM transmission are:
- Very high frequency waves (VHF) (typically 30–300 MHz).
- More complex and expensive circuitry needed.
- Takes up a large band of frequency.
- Used for radio requiring high quality music transmission.
- Works on a shorter line-of-sight principle, hence used by local radio.
- Immune to electrical noise and some atmospheric conditions, although the signal strength can be influenced by reflection from buildings and hills, creating dead spots.

The future of radio

Radio on a chip

Many small radio receivers are built around dedicated integrated circuits (ICs) that only require the addition of a small number of extra components. The ICs usually contain the demodulating circuitry,

> **AQA Examiner's tip**
> You do not need to know about the future of radio for your exam.

filtering and amplification in one package. Although the ULN2204A and the TDA 7000 IC's have been around for some time they give an indication as to what is available on the market. Figure **B** shows the TDA 7000 radio IC circuit.

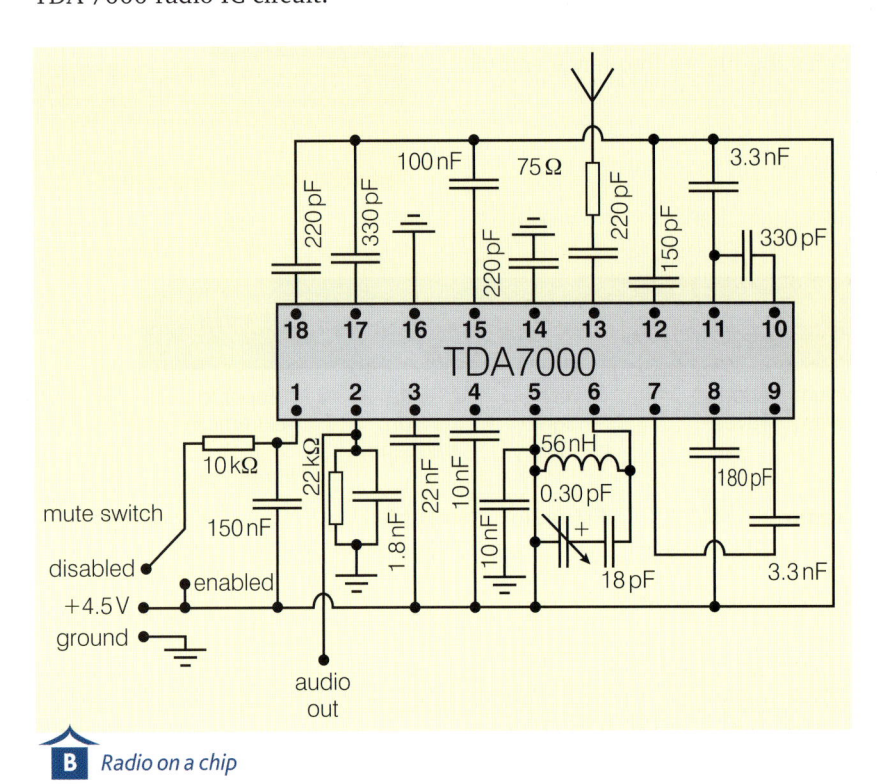

B *Radio on a chip*

DAB radio

Digital audio broadcasting (DAB) is already here and works by the program being split up into small packets of digital information which are then transmitted in multiple bursts. Each packet contains coded information so that when it is received, the receiver can put the packets back into the correct order.

Advantages of DAB:

The same frequency can be used across the country – no retuning from station to station is needed.
- All the old AM and FM stations can be transmitted free from interference, as well as many new stations, due to the large capacity of the system.
- Data can also be transmitted so that that information about the station and programme arrive together and can be displayed on a screen.

Chapter 12 Radio systems

Summary

Radio waves are part of the electromagnetic spectrum.

Radio waves are used to carry audio information using modulation techniques.

AM stands for amplitude modulation. This means a change in wave amplitude encodes the information.

FM stands for frequency modulation. This means a change in frequency encodes the information.

A simple radio receiver contains the following subsystems: aerial, tuned circuit, demodulator, amplifier and loudspeaker.

A good quality receiver will be able to pick out the required radio station (selectivity) and will be able to detect distant radio stations (sensitivity).

Questions

1. Complete each of the statements below by using either the word *radio* or *audio*.

   ……………………… waves can be detected by an aerial.
   ……………………. waves are rich in information.
   ……………………… waves travel at the speed of light.
   A loudspeaker gives out …………………… waves.
   ……………………. waves are part of the electromagnetic spectrum.

2. Which two techniques are used to place audio information onto a radio wave? Draw a diagram to show one of the techniques.

3. Explain why the radio wave is often referred to as the carrier wave.

4. Explain the part played by the tuned circuit in a simple radio receiver.

5. State one advantage and one disadvantage of using an FM system rather than an AM system.

6. A particular radio receiver is said to lack sensitivity. Explain what this means and state one simple way of improving this.

13 Programmed systems

13.1 Microcontrollers

What is a microcontroller?

Microcontrollers are computers on a single IC, complete with memory and all the circuits needed for input and output. There are microcontrollers in mobile phones, MP3 players, chip-and-pin debit cards, televisions, electric toasters and, in fact, in almost all electronic goods. Millions of microcontrollers are produced every year and so they are relatively cheap.

Programming

Microcontrollers are controlled by a program. A **program** is set of instructions that tell the microcontroller how to work. It is usually much faster and easier for an engineer to write a program for a microcontroller than to design a circuit to do the same job. The engineer writes the program on a desktop computer or laptop and tries it out on the screen until it is working as needed. When the program is ready, a special programmer is attached to the computer and the microcontroller is connected to the programmer. The computer program is now loaded into the microcontroller and stored in the program memory. The microcontroller is now put in a circuit and will do what it has been programmed to do.

Pros and cons

The program in the microcontroller can be altered so that the way it operates can be changed. This means that manufacturers can change the way a circuit operates before it leaves the factory. The equipment can then be updated if a fault is found, or a new feature is needed, and equipment is not wasted. Users can sometimes update their equipment at home by downloading new software and reprogramming the microcontroller in their electronics with an updated program. The program memory is often a special kind of memory called **flash memory** so reprogramming is sometimes called **flashing**. The software in a microcontroller that makes it operate is usually called **firmware**. If a circuit needs to be very fast, it needs to be designed to do the job. Microcontrollers are not as fast as specially designed circuits.

Microcontrollers have made things smarter because it is easier to automate things with programs. People used to write down phone numbers, but with microcontrollers, the phone can store the telephone number and do the dialling automatically.

Because it is fast and cheap to produce microcontroller based systems, new electronics equipment is being produced all the time. This means that equipment is soon out of date. Some people worry about the amount of waste produced by constantly buying new electronic goods and throwing away equipment that is not very old.

Objectives

In this section you will learn:

what a microcontroller is

where microcontrollers are used

some of the effects of microcontrollers on society.

Key terms

Microcontroller: computers on a single IC complete with memory and all the circuits needed for input and output.

Program: sequence of instructions that a computer can interpret and carry out.

Chapter 13 Programmed systems 101

13.2 Converting between analogue and digital signals

Microcontrollers are digital devices; they use only 1s and 0s. Signals which are only high or low can be connected straight to the inputs of the microcontroller like switches and simple sensors. The outputs of the microcontroller can be used to turn things on and off like LEDs, motors and bulbs.

ADC

Sometimes an **analogue signal** like the sound signal from a microphone or a voltage from a temperature sensor may be connected to a microcontroller. To connect an analogue signal to a microcontroller an analogue-to-digital converter (**ADC**) must be used. An ADC is a circuit that turns the analogue voltage into **digital signals** (0s and 1s). The simplest analogue-to-digital converter is the comparator.

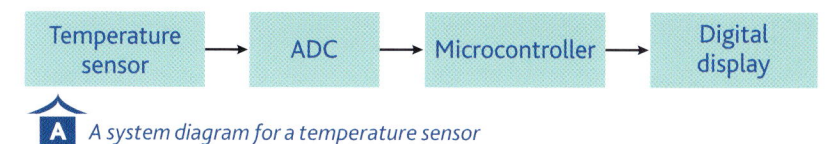

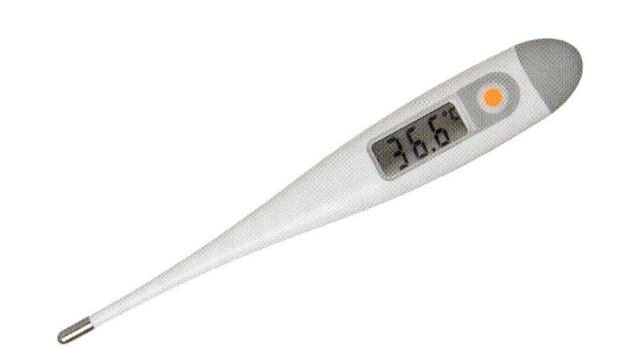

Temperature sensor → ADC → Microcontroller → Digital display

A A system diagram for a temperature sensor

B A digital thermometer

DAC

To produce an analogue signal from a microcontroller, a digital-to-analogue converter (**DAC**) must be used. When we want to use a microcontroller to play music, we use a DAC to connect the microcontroller to a loudspeaker or headphones. The DAC converts the 1s and 0s into a voltage.

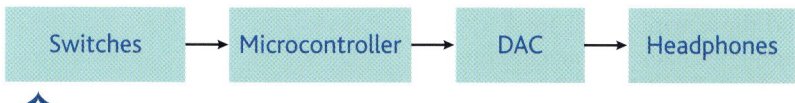

Switches → Microcontroller → DAC → Headphones

C A system diagram for an MP3 player.

Objectives

In this section you will learn:

to understand the need for conversion between analogue and digital signals

when an ADC is used

when a DAC is used.

Key terms

Analogue signal: signal that can have any value between a minimum and a maximum.

Digital signal: signal that can have only two states, high voltage for 1 and low voltage for 0.

links

You first met the ADC when looking at the comparator circuit in Chapter 9.

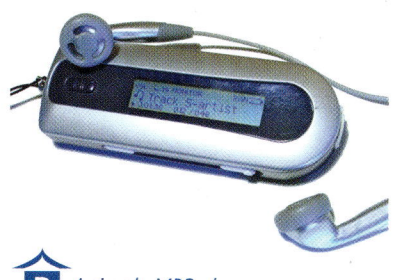

D A simple MP3 player

13.3 Flowchart diagrams

Flowchart symbols

Programs for microcontrollers and other sequences of events can be described using **flowchart diagrams**. A flowchart breaks a problem down into small steps and shows the order of the steps. There are special symbols used in a flowchart which you need to learn; the shape shows the type of function of each step.

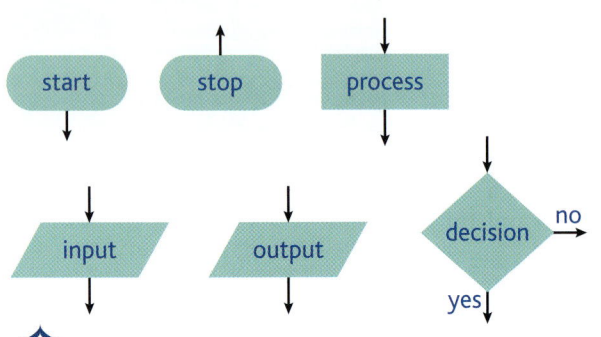

A *Flowchart symbols*

Objectives

In this section you will learn:

how to use and interpret flowchart diagrams.

Key terms

Flowchart diagram: a diagram which uses special shapes and arrows to describe a program or other process in a sequence of instructions.

The start and stop symbols are called **terminal boxes** because the program starts or ends here. The **decision box** always contains a question which can only have a yes or no answer. An **input** symbol shows where information goes into the system, and an **output** symbol shows where information comes out of the system - normally turning something on or off. The **process** symbol shows things that happen inside the system like timing and counting. People sometimes find it difficult to choose between a process and an input or output. Sensors and switches are always inputs. Displays and things that make light, noise or movement are outputs. Timing and counting and other things where the information stays in the system are processes.

B *A flowchart diagram for a car alarm*

An example

The best way to understand flowcharts is with an example. Figure **B** shows the flowchart for a car alarm. The system keeps checking a motion sensor. When motion is detected the alarm sounds for 2 minutes and then turns off, and the system goes back to checking the motion sensor. The line which goes from the "no" at the decision box back to "Get information from the sensor" is called a **loop**, because it makes the program go back to an earlier point in the program.

Chapter 13 Programmed systems

Summary

Microcontrollers are cheap, quick and easy to program.

The way microcontrollers work can easily be changed but they are not as fast as digital circuits made from logic gates and other digital components.

Microcontrollers are digital devices, so an analogue to digital converter (ADC) is needed to connect an analogue input device to a microcontroller. A comparator is a simple ADC.

A digital to analogue converter (DAC) is needed to connect a microcontroller to an analogue output device.

The program in a microcontroller can be described with a flowchart which uses a shaped box for each step. You should now know which shape to use for each box.

Questions

1. Find an example of each kind of a symbol (terminal box, input, output, decision, process) in the car alarm program in Figure **B**.
2. Draw the flowchart for a smoke alarm.
3. Draw the flowchart for a coin-operated coffee machine.
4. What do you have in your home that contains microcontrollers?
5. Write down three benefits of microcontrollers.
6. Do you think microcontrollers have caused any problems in society?
7. Draw the block diagram of a light meter that contains a microcontroller.
8. Draw the block diagram for a digital voice recorder that can record and play back spoken messages.

14 The Controlled Assessment

14.1 Introducing the Controlled Assessment

Modern microelectronics is one of the most important areas of applied science which with thoughtful application can bring real benefit to society. However, it may also be argued that there can be some serious disadvantages as well, when the full range of social, economic and environmental issues are considered.

As an applied science, electronics underpins a significant portion of our modern technological development and it is important to understand how it can be used to solve problems.

The controlled assessment allows you to participate in this development by using the knowledge and skills you have acquired to solve problems where the most appropriate solution is through Electronics.

The assessment can be thought of as fulfilling the following objectives:
- To allow you to experience the full analysis, design, build and evaluation cycle when proposing a solution to a perceived problem.
- To allow you to demonstrate a range of research and practical skills.
- To allow you to develop communication skills for the work you undertake. (Electronic engineers often work as part of a multi-disciplinary team and the clear communication of your ideas to others is important.)

How does the Controlled Assessment fit into the specification?

The Controlled Assessment is the only coursework component in the specification. It is worth 50 marks and this accounts for 25% of the whole examination.

There are 22 assessment points and you should use the grid in the specification to keep track of how many points you have covered. This will give you a good idea of what your final mark should be.

The whole exercise is intended to take up to about 30 hours of class time, which includes time to write the report.

What are the basics I need?

You need access to some basic kit before you can start your project. The following is suggested:
- Regulated dc power supply (variable or switchable in the range 0–15 V) or batteries.
- Breadboard.
- Access to connecting wire, basic tools such as wire strippers/cutters/snipe nose pliers together with the main discrete components covered in the course.
- A project diary book, where all ideas/references/circuits/modifications and tests can be recorded. This will provide the main resource for writing your report later.
- Research material – books, magazines and/or access to the internet.

> **Objectives**
>
> In this chapter you will learn:
>
> to understand the major aspects of the project development cycle
>
> to understand the place of the Controlled Assessment within the specification
>
> to appreciate the basic equipment needed before starting the development
>
> to understand the planning process
>
> to understand the realisation process
>
> to understand the testing and evaluation process.

14.2 Getting to grips with design

The task of developing a solution to a problem can appear daunting. This is usually because you want to build something which is too complex and you are unable to understand how the system can be broken down into simpler recognisable subsystems. It is important to identify problems that can be solved by using the electronics covered in the course, or at least not to go too far beyond the course.

What have I learned?

Since the most basic system will inevitably have three subsystems (Input, Process and Output), a good place to start is to make your own list of the components and subsystems from the course and place them into the appropriate categories.

Activity

1 Identifying subsystems

Table A gives you a start and you should complete and extend this to cover as many components and subsystems from the course as you can. Note: there is no preferred order to the table, just make sure that the subsystems covered in the course go into the appropriate columns.

A *Table of subsystems*

input	process	output
pressure pad switch	1 of 10 counter	light emitting diode
-------	----------	
--------	astable	------
light dependent resistor	---------	buzzer
thermistor	monostable	-------

How do I start designing?

The main point is to understand how to read a system diagram which is made from a number of subsystems. As a starting point, try reading across a line in your table to see if the system might do anything useful. The first line taken from Table **A** is done for you and is shown in Figure **B**.

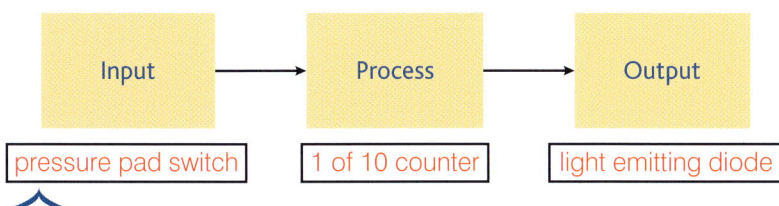

Input → Process → Output

pressure pad switch | 1 of 10 counter | light emitting diode

B *Reading a system diagram*

This system could quite easily do a useful job. Each time the switch is pressed by someone standing on it, the counter records the pulse and the next LED lights up. This could be adapted to finding out how many people have gone into a room, e.g. at a museum. However, you may feel that the practicalities of a pressure pad in this situation would be unrealistic and you may opt for a different type of sensor.

> **Activity**
>
> **2 Subsystems**
>
> Using the table you have completed try the following tasks.
>
> a Scan each line of your table to see if you have a system that could perform a useful job.
>
> b Take any one subsystem from each of input, process and output from Table **A** and use them together to produce a solution to a problem – discuss this with others, as a fresh mind might spot a problem with the system you propose.
>
> c When you have some confidence with using three subsystems, extend the idea to more than three, e.g. using more than one input, process or output to perform more complex tasks.

> **AQA Examiner's tip**
>
> There is no upper limit to the number of subsystems you may use but you should remember that there are no extra marks for the complexity of the design. A suggested upper limit would be five to six subsystems.

Designing for a problem

This is where the real designing starts. Instead of thinking of a use for a collection of subsystems, in the real world you would be asked to design a solution to a real problem. You should now try to think of things you would like your system to do and use your knowledge to design a system diagram on paper to achieve this.

> **Activity**
>
> **3 Solving problems**
>
> Draw system diagrams for solving the following problems.
>
> Here are some ideas to try. (There will often be more than one acceptable solution.)
>
> - When a shadow passes across a detector, an audible alarm sounds for a given length of time.
> - A small electromagnetic relay is activated when two switches are pushed together.
> - When the room lighting becomes dim, a flashing warning light is activated.
> - A row of LEDs are to form a running arrow head which is to act as a motorway warning sign.

> **AQA Examiner's tip**
>
> Remember, if it does not work on paper, it will never work as a practical system. If it works on paper – there is a chance it could work when you build it.

14.3 Planning

What type of problems should I try to solve?

There are a number of things you should and should not do in order to help you to gain the maximum benefit from the assessment mark scheme.

Things you should do

- Do solve problems from areas of society that allow you to produce a solution using your own knowledge.
- Do consider the following areas as a rich source of ideas. (There are other lists given in the specification.)
  1. **Security** – triggered alarms/coded locks, etc.
  2. **Electronic games/novelty systems** – dice, live wire game, reaction timer/snap, etc.
  3. **Model a real system** – traffic lights/car park systems/kitchen timer/auto porch light/simple IR remote control, etc.
- Do use a subsystem from your notes/textbook or other reference which can easily be altered to fit your own overall design requirements.
- Do use realistic modelling to allow time for frequent testing. For example, let 1 s represent 1 min in a kitchen timer or 5 s for a traffic light.

Things you should not do

- Don't use mains electricity in any part of your project.
- Don't rely on software-driven devices as only hardware is assessed.
- Don't select an off-the-shelf project from a magazine/book/internet as it is unlikely to support the planning/design marks and could make detailed testing difficult.
- Don't go outside the syllabus unless you have detailed knowledge of how the component works.
- Don't allow yourself to cross the line between the requirements for the course and the taking on of an overly complex project.

At this level, both **radio** and **audio effect** type projects are likely to lead to a number of problems and are best avoided. In both areas, you may struggle to put in enough of your own design, generate specifications or be able to identify sufficient subsystems that can be independently tested. This will inevitably affect your assessment potential. Radio work in particular requires careful compliance with current communication legislation and breadboards are not always the best construction base for such work. Audio effect systems such as wah-wah effects for guitars are difficult to give specifications for and difficult to test.

How do I get planning marks?

When you have decided on a problem to solve or identified a useful function you wish to build, it should be set in context (where and how the circuit will bring about an improvement to our lives).

Block diagram

Draw out a system diagram. This may start as a block diagram showing just three simple subsystems (input, process and output). Don't forget to put connecting lines with arrows to show which way the information flows.

The block diagram may be developed to show more detail (additional subsystems and signal shapes) as shown in Figure **A**.

System diagram 1

Input → Process → Output

System diagram 2

Input
LDR
pot chain
→ Process
555
monostable
→ Output
buzzer

A *The development of a system diagram*

By developing the diagram in this way it will help you to remember that the process block must be able to accept the type of signal it will get from the previous block. In the example given, knowledge of the signal required to trigger a monostable will determine which way around the LDR chain in the previous block must be built.

Research

Use your notes, books, magazines, catalogues and the internet to gain the information you need. The research you do can be used in a number of ways to support marks awarded in the assessment stage.

Typical areas are:

Gathering technical detail

It is essential that you are able to say where the technical detail you are using has come from. Full references will be expected. Examples of technical information include:

- Obtaining pin-out diagrams for ICs.
- Obtaining a parameter for a component, e.g. typical forward current for an LED or the operating voltage for a miniature electric motor.
- Gathering the formula needed for a calculation, e.g. time period for a monostable.

Reviewing possible alternative subsystems

You must give some consideration to subsystems that would perform a similar function to the one you are going to use. Don't forget to give a reason for your choice. Some examples of alternatives are:

- A buzzer can be used as the audible output, but if you want to have control over the frequency then it would be best to opt for an astable driving a loudspeaker.

> **AQA Examiner's tip**
>
> Having identified a title and aim and produced a detailed systems diagram, this is a good stage to explain to your supervisor how you think your system will work. A more experienced eye may well help identify defects in your plan which may need correcting before you start to build.

- A microprocessor could replace the whole of the processing system, but your lack of knowledge may preclude this.
- You may be surprised at how many ways there are of making an astable in a circuit – some are too complex, others give poor pulse shapes for use with digital circuits, although this can be overcome.

Quantitative specifications

In order that the project can be tested/evaluated later, you need to have some numerical (quantitative) specifications that you can measure your project against. It is intended that the measurement requires a meter. A DMM, CRO or similar should be used.

With any numerical specification, a sensible tolerance should be given, e.g. ± 10%, or a range (9 V down to 6 V).

Typical specifications might be:
- The voltage range that will allow the project to function normally.
- The time period that an alarm is on for.
- The frequency at which the lights flash.
- The light level that will trigger the alarm.
- The current drawn on standby.
- The current drawn when active.

Examples of numerical specifications that are not electronic in nature and should not be used are:
- The project lights three LEDs.
- The alarm can be heard 5 m away.
- The alarm has two inputs.

A practical investigation

When you are at the planning stage, you don't always know exactly how you want your system to perform. Questions that are often asked at this stage are:
- How fast should the dice pattern change to make it look realistic?
- What frequency should an alarm have to make it annoying?
- How dark should it be before the emergency light comes on?
- How long should I allow myself to get out of the house after setting the alarm?
- Will the counter actually detect pulses from that sensor?

These questions can often only be answered by sitting down with a signal generator and amplifier or with a stop watch or light meter, and carrying out an investigation so that you can decide what is acceptable to you. (Don't forget to record what you have done.)

AQA Examiner's tip
Marks cannot be gained for investigations carried out in a virtual environment on CAD packages. Make sure you provide sufficient evidence to prove that a real practical investigation was performed.

14.4 Can I get started?

Of course you can - this is the bit you have been waiting for. Just remember that the better your planning and research has been, the fewer nasty surprises you will have when you start to build.

The golden rules for building

- Based on your most comprehensive block diagram, number the blocks in sequence and think how best to set them out on the breadboard so that each subsystem has plenty of space and is able to follow in sequence. If you do not adopt a good plan, the final circuit will look messy and disorganised.
- Starting with block one, build and test it. Remember that even for a simple potential divider type of circuit, recording the voltage at the mid-point would constitute a test. If you expected a falling pulse when a shadow passes across the LDR then this should be measurable.
- Identify any faults and correct them – retest if necessary and sketch a circuit diagram with component values.
- Move onto subsystem 2 and repeat the procedure. Try to test the subsystem as an independent block then test blocks 1 and 2 together.
- Identify faults/correct/retest and sketch a circuit diagram with component values.
- Continue the procedure through each subsystem.

If you follow the build and test procedure, you will know where the fault lies when a problem occurs.

What happens if I get really stuck?

You should discuss the progress of your project at regular intervals with your supervisor – even if things are going well. If there are problems, you should be able to contribute to isolating the problem through the build and test regime, even if the solution to the problem is outside your sphere of experience. Supervisors are asked to provide sufficient help to make it possible for you to make progress, but they will record any significant help given.

Common problems

The most common problems found during the building phase can be split into two categories: those relating to the mechanics of building and those relating to the design of the circuit.

Problems associated with the mechanics of building:

- Insufficient bare wire on the end of the jump leads leading to poor contact inside the breadboard.
- Careless placing of wires in the breadboard grid.
- Polarised components not correctly orientated.
- Some unused pins on chips may not have been connected to one of the power rails as suggested on the data sheet for that component.

> **AQA Examiner's tip**
>
> When building, keep the wiring quite neat as you go along and colour code your wires if possible. Suggested colours:
>
> Power rails and supplies to chips – **Red** (+) and **Black** (−)
>
> Depending on the background colour of the breadboard – **White** can be used to identify the signal route from subsystem to subsystem.
>
> All other wires around chips/potential chains etc. – **Any other single colour**.

> **AQA Examiner's tip**
>
> Using a protected LED on the output of some subsystems gives a quick visual indication of the status of that subsystem and can aid fault finding.

Problems associated with the design:

The main problem here is when subsystems are not performing as expected when connected together. These can be difficult for some candidates to solve. Three such common problems are:

- The need to provide current buffering to an output stage, e.g. CMOS logic gates cannot source enough current for most output devices and may need a transducer driver. This may not have been spotted at the design stage.
- Due to a problem with the original design, a 555 monostable acting as a second stage may be triggered, but does not turn off. It may be that a simple first stage is only providing a single edge pulse rather than one that has a return edge. (An R–C based pulse shaper may be needed here.)
- Some digital pulses from sensors are not always clean enough to satisfy counting chips and this leads to spurious counting. Schmitt triggers and anti-bounce circuits brought in as extra subsystems can help clean up the information.

What must I do when I have finished building the system?

By using the build and test regime, you will already have dealt with most of the problems as you have gone along. Now you need to evaluate your design by checking that:

- The sequence of operation is correct.
- The numerical parameters (specifications) you gave in your plan have been measured and that the initial specifications and actual measurements have been recorded in a boxed table that has suitable headings and units. (Don't forget to record the measuring instrument used.)
- If any specification (numerical or otherwise) does not achieve the standard you required, you should make a change or suggest a modification that would make the project perform more accurately to the original specifications.

14.5 The written report

If you have been keeping a good project diary that has been updated each time you have done some lab work, then you will already have much of the technical detail for the report to hand.

The report is best written to reflect the chronological order in which the project was tackled and should contain significant aspects of the planning, building, testing and evaluation to show the full development cycle. It is best done on computer as a word document so that you can use a spell and grammar check. It is also easier to put in pictures and to change the layout of your report as it develops.

One approach would be as follows:

- Introduce the idea (title, non-technical explanation of the function, context).
- Develop the full system diagram.
- Discuss alternatives, practical investigation and references.
- Number the subsystems and dedicate a full page to each subsystem For each subsystem give:
    1. A brief introduction to the role of the subsystem.
    2. Calculations of component values or function values, e.g. time period or frequency.
    3. A circuit diagram with components and values and any references.
    4. A description of any tests done with values, instruments and technique used.
    5. A description of any faults noted and how they were corrected.
    6. A clear indication on your circuit diagram of the signal leaving the subsystem so that it can be shown on the next page coming into the next subsystem.

Repeat the processes **1** to **5** using a new page for each subsystem.

- Do an evaluation by comparing the original and final specifications (use a table to show numerical values).
- Discuss any modifications needed to make the final system perform to the original specifications better.
- Gather all references and acknowledgements you have used – these should already be indicated in your text at the point of use.
- Provide a photograph of the full final circuit (this should be a close-up so that detail of the components and overall wiring and circuit design can be seen, as in Figure **A**.

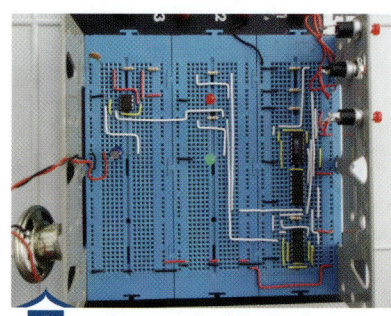

A A photograph of the final system

Circuit diagrams and pictures

Some circuit diagrams may be difficult to draw on a word processing package and CAD based diagrams may not allow you to show the detail you need. There is still something to be said for drawing your circuit diagrams on plain paper and then scanning or sticking them into the report. (Don't forget to make photocopies in case you have to rewrite a page.) Photographs may be used to show the development of the project but **cannot** be used as a replacement for a circuit diagram.

Your report just needs the finishing touches – front cover and pages numbering – and then it is ready for handing in.

> **AQA Examiner's tip**
> Check the 22 marking points within your report – how many did you get?

Examination-style questions

1 **(a)** What component can be used to obtain a safe low voltage from the mains supply? *(1 mark)*

(b) Name two components that can be used to protect a circuit from a current overload. *(2 marks)*

(c) State the colours of these wires in a three-pin mains plug.
  (i) Earth
  (ii) Live
  (iii) Neutral *(3 marks)*

(d) To help prevent accidents while working on electronics projects, state two measures that students should take. *(2 marks)*

(e) State two effects on the human body of a large electric current. *(2 marks)*

AQA, 2007

2 Figure 1 shows a mains power supply unit which has a metal case.

Figure 1

(a) **(i)** Name the part labelled **A**.
  (ii) Name the mains wire which **must** be connected to part **A**. *(2 marks)*

(b) **(i)** Name the wire which **must** be connected to the metal case.
  (ii) What is the function of the grommet labelled **E**? *(2 marks)*

(c) **(i)** Which labelled part is the mains fuse?
  (ii) Which labelled part is the circuit breaker?
  (iii) State a difference between a fuse and a circuit breaker. *(3 marks)*

AQA, 2002

3 The following statements are concerned with electrical safety. Fill in the missing words.

(a) A fuse is a piece of wire which melts if too much ………… flows through it.

(b) The fuse is always in the ………… wire which is coloured ………… in the lead from the appliance to the plug.

(c) It is dangerous to fit a fuse with too ………… a value.

(d) Handling electrical equipment with wet hands is very dangerous because water ………… the resistance of the skin.

(e) Inside an appliance such as a washing machine the ………… wire is connected to the metal case of the appliance.

(f) One advantage of a Residual Current Device over a fuse is that a smaller flow of ………… to earth will disconnect the supply.

(g) A component which may still be dangerous after an appliance has been disconnected from the mains is a ………… . This component is dangerous because it can store a lethal ………… *(10 marks)*

AQA, 2001

114 Examination-style questions

4 A block diagram of an automatic porch light is shown in Figure 2.

light sensor → comparator → monostable → driver → lamp

Figure 2

(a) Which block represents
  (i) an input?
  (ii) an output?
  (iii) an analogue to digital converter? *(3 marks)*
(b) In which block could
  (i) an op-amp be found?
  (ii) an LDR be found?
  (iii) a 555 IC be found? *(3 marks)*
(c) Complete the gaps in this description of the operation of the system. When the light level falls, the output of the .... goes low and triggers the .... This gives a high voltage signal to the .... which switches on the .... for a period of .... *(4 marks)*

AQA, 2008

5 A resistor, switch, LED and power supply are connected as shown in Figure 3.

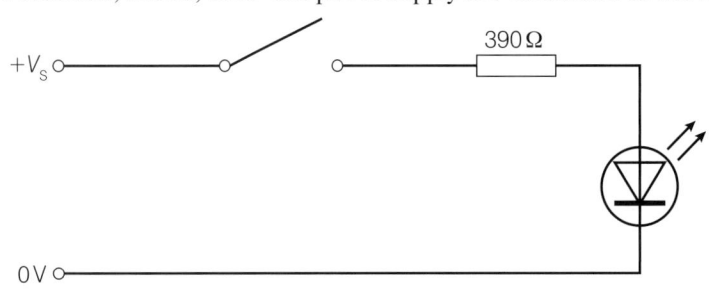

Figure 3

(a) How are the resistor and LED arranged? *(1 mark)*
(b) (i) Draw on the circuit diagram where you would connect an ammeter to measure the current through the resistor and LED.
  (ii) The LED is found to be too dim. What is the cause of this?
  (iii) Draw on the circuit diagram where you would connect an extra resistor to increase the current through the LED.
  (iv) State an alternative way of changing the circuit to increase the brightness of the LED. *(5 marks)*
(c) Write down the colour code of the resistor shown in the circuit diagram above if it had 5% tolerance.
  1st band: ....   2nd band: ....
  3rd band: ....   4th band: .... *(4 marks)*

AQA, 2001

6 (a) Complete these truth tables for AND and OR gates.

AND		
A	B	output
0	0	
0	1	
1	0	
1	1	

OR		
A	B	output
0	0	
0	1	
1	0	
1	1	

Two computers are connected to the same printer using the circuit shown in Figure 4.

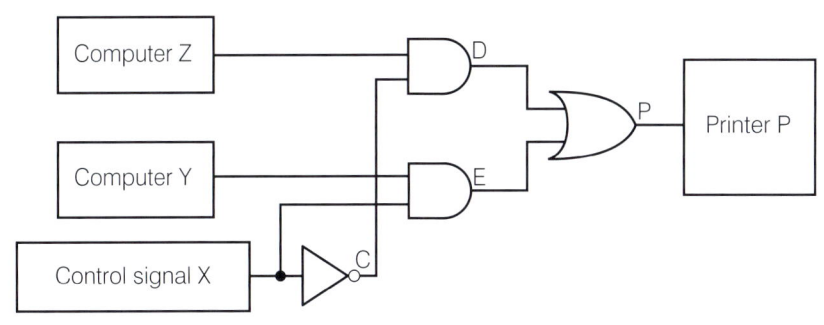

Figure 4

(b) Complete this truth table for the whole system.

X	Y	Z	C	D	E	P
0	0	0				
0	0	1				
0	1	0				
0	1	1				
1	0	0				
1	0	1				
1	1	0				
1	1	1				

(c) Explain how the control signal is used to select which computer is connected to the printer.

(10 marks)

AQA, 2003

7 (a) Label the leads on the n-channel MOSFET in Figure 5.

(3 marks)

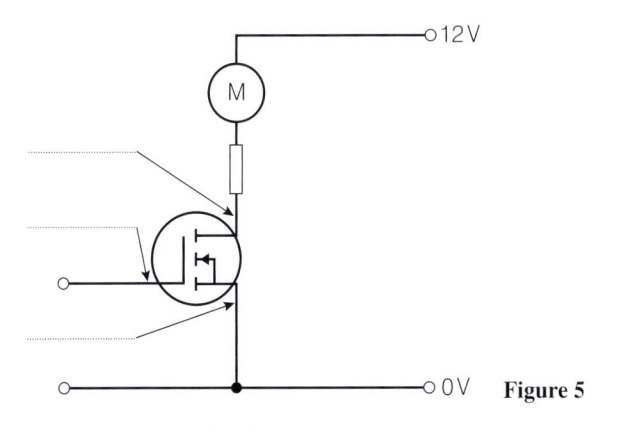

Figure 5

(b) The MOSFET is used to switch an electric motor, which has a resistor in series with it.
  (i) State the function of the resistor in this circuit.
  (ii) On switching the motor on, the current through the resistor is 3 A and the voltage across it is 6 V. Calculate the value of resistor required.
  (iii) Calculate the power dissipated by the resistor under these conditions. *(5 marks)*
(c) Why does the MOSFET need no series input resistor? *(1 mark)*

AQA, 1998

8 When someone approaches a front door, a light is automatically switched on for 30 s.
  (a) (i) A 555 timer IC connected as a monostable produces the time delay. Complete Figure 6 to show how the 555 timer should be connected. Add **two** capacitors, **one** resistor and the wire links needed.

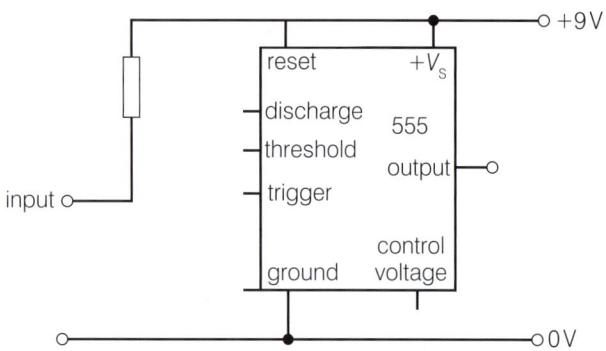

Figure 6

  (ii) The timing capacitor and resistor have values of 100 μF and 270 kΩ, respectively. Show that they produce the required time interval. Your answer must be corrected to the nearest second. *(9 marks)*

AQA, 2003

9 (a) A D-type flip-flop is used as a latch.
  (i) Name and label the **two** inputs with their full names.
  (ii) Label the ouput. *(3 marks)*

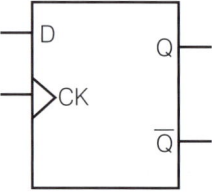

Figure 7

(b) Describe the operation of a 4013 type D-type flip-flop. *(3 marks)*
(c) The D-type flip-flop can also function as a frequency divider. Complete Figure 8 to show how two D-type flip-flops can divide an input signal by a factor of four. Label the input and output of your circuit and draw the wire links required.

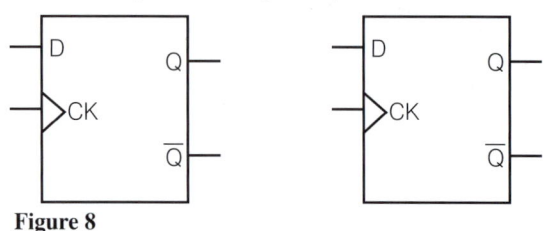

Figure 8

(4 marks)

AQA, 2007

10 A fridge alarm sounds if the temperature is too high. It uses the following circuit.

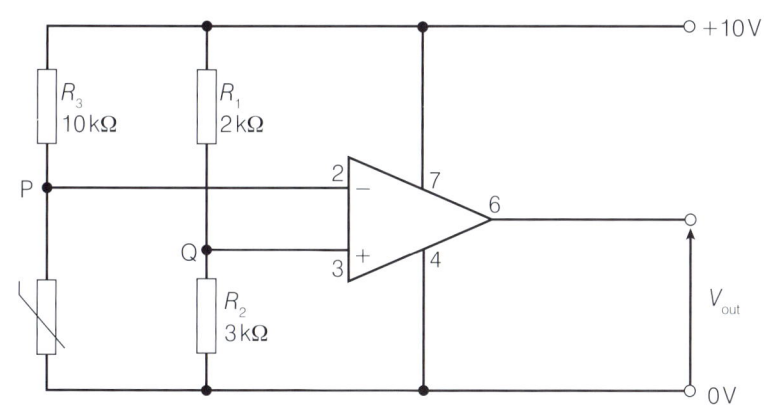

Figure 9

(a) (i) Calculate the combined resistance of resistors, R_1 and R_2.
 (ii) Calculate the voltage at **Q**.
 (iii) State the voltage at **P** just at the point when V_{out} changes.
 (iv) Calculate the resistance of the thermistor when V_{out} changes.
 (v) What will happen to V_{out} when the temperature of the thermistor changes from being very cold to warm? *(6 marks)*

(b) This circuit is built on breadboard. Complete the layout diagram and label the resistors. (The pin connection numbers for the op-amp are indicated in Figure 10.) *(9 marks)*

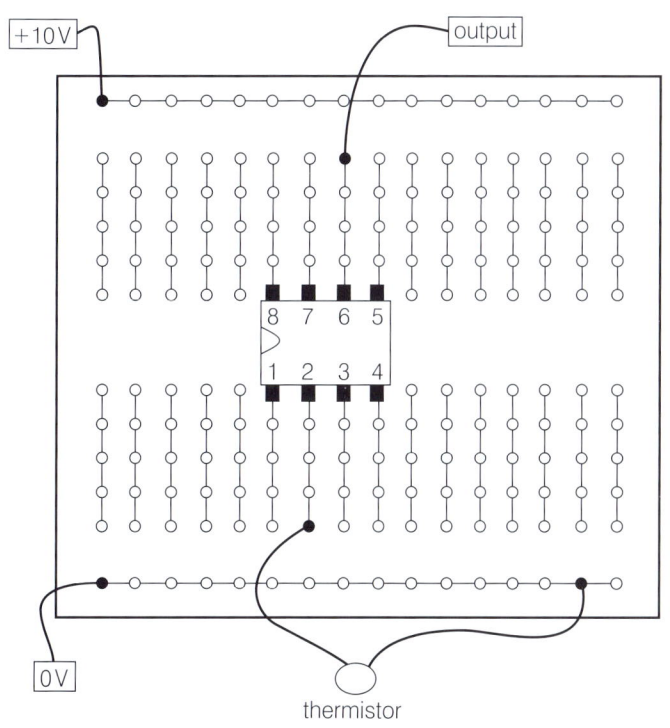

Figure 10

AQA, 2005

11 A student decides to build an audio amplifier using an integrated circuit (IC) which they have not seen before. They use the circuit diagram in Figure 11, which shows the pin numbers of the integrated circuit, to construct the amplifier on prototyping board.

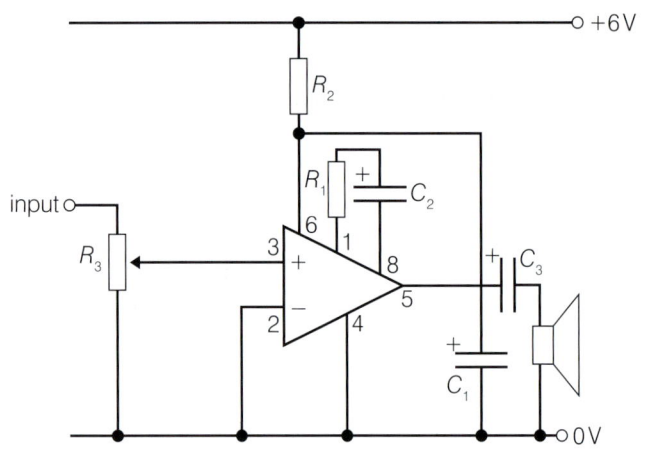

Figure 11

(a) (i) What is the name of the type of component which is labelled R_3?
   (ii) What is the function of R_3 in this amplifier circuit?
   (iii) R_2 has a value of 10 Ω and a tolerance of 5%. Label the colour of the bands in Figure 12.

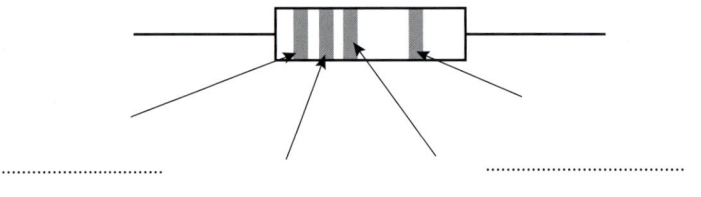

(6 marks)

Figure 12

AQA, 2008

12 Information can be transmitted as either an analogue or a digital signal.

(a) (i) What type of signal is shown in Figure 13?

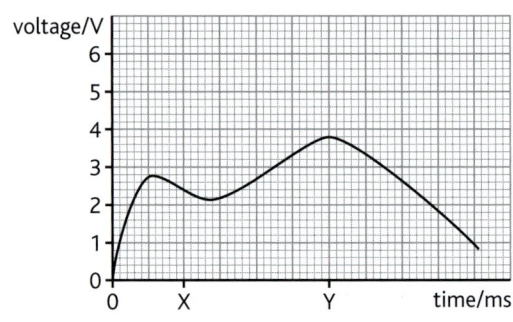

Figure 13

(ii) What is the value of the amplitude of this signal at points X and Y in the diagram?
Value at X is ....
Value at Y is ....

(iii) Signals in cables are subject to *noise*.
What is noise and how might it be caused?

(iv) These signals have suffered noise interference:

Analogue signal

Digital signal

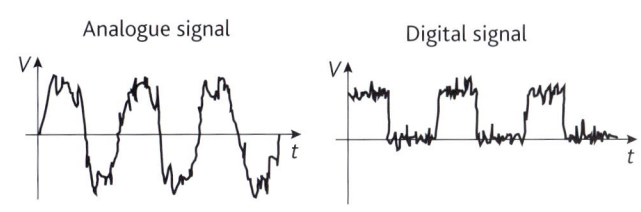

Figure 14

In which signal (analogue or digital) is the noise most damaging?
(v) Explain why the noise need not be as damaging for one signal as for the other.
(vi) Name a type of cable that can be used to join subsystems together to minimise noise. *(12 marks)*

(b) In an analogue to digital converter, the level of the signal is represented by a binary number.
(i) How many different levels can be represented by a four-bit binary number?
(ii) Why would an analogue to digital converter, which used eight bits when sampling the level, be better than a four-bit converter? *(4 marks)*

AQA, 2008

13 A power supply contains a transformer which has an output with a peak value of 12 V.
(a) (i) The frequency of the output is 50 Hz. Calculate the time period in seconds.
(ii) State the time period in milliseconds.
(iii) Draw the trace you would expect to see if you connected the 12 V_{peak} output to an oscilloscope with the following settings.

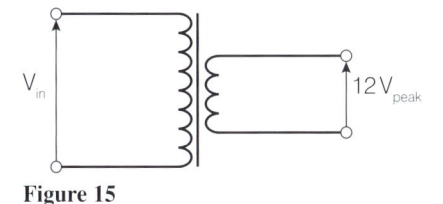

Figure 15

The Y sensitivity is set to 5 V per cm
The timebase is set to ms per cm

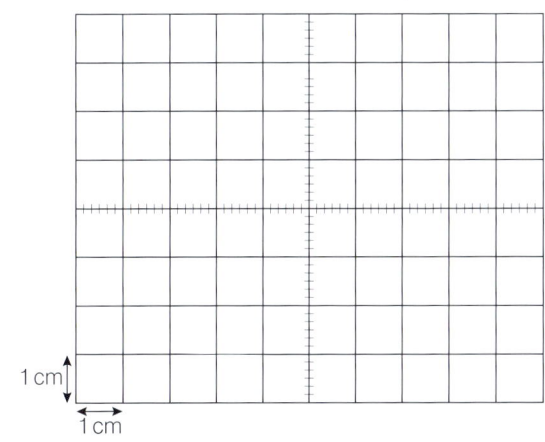

1 cm
1 cm

Figure 16

(iv) Calculate the rms value of the output voltage from the transformer.

(b) (i) The transformer is part of a power supply which produces a rectified, smoothed and regulated voltage output and contains a fuse. Label each of the four boxes with the name of an appropriate component.

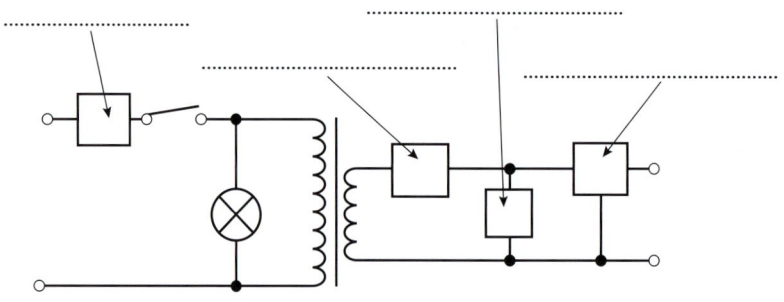

Figure 17

(ii) The power supply has a maximum power consumption of 80 W and operates from 230 V mains. Calculate the mains current.

(iii) Draw a circle around the best value for the fuse in this power supply.
100 mA   250 mA   1 A   5 A   13 A

(c) The power supply is connected to the mains using a three-pin plug. Label the names and colours of the wires in the plug.

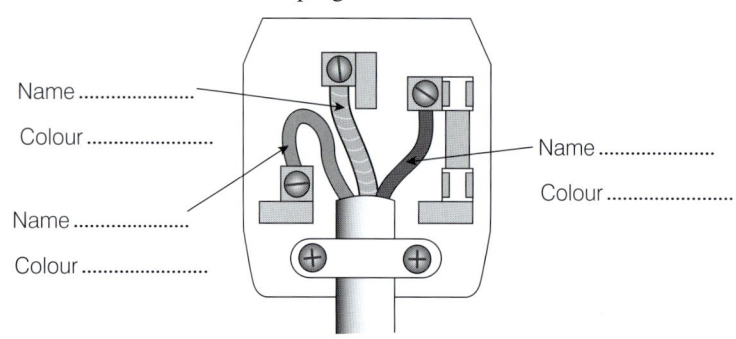

Name ....
Colour ....

Name ....
Colour ....

Name ....
Colour ....

Figure 18

AQA, 2005

14 The flowchart describes the operation of a simple house intruder alarm. Some of the flowchart symbols have been left out.

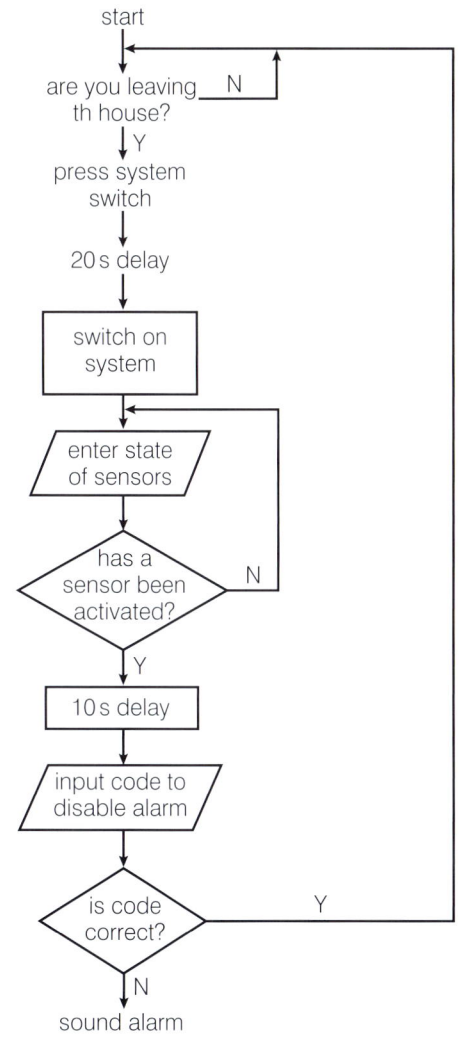

Figure 19

(a) Draw the correct flowchart symbols at **five** places where they are missing on the diagram. *(5 marks)*

(b) Label on the flowchart:
a decision box   **an input box**   **a loop**
an output box   **a process box**
(5 marks)

(c) An intruder, who does not know the correct code in order to disable the alarm, enters the house after the alarm has been set.
Using the flowchart in part (**a**), describe the sequence of events that will occur. *(5 marks)*

(d) Using the lower part of the flowchart in part (**a**) as a guide, draw a new flowchart that would allow two incorrect attempts at entering the code before sounding the alarm when a third incorrect attempt is made. Start your flowchart from the 10s delay box. *(5 marks)*

AQA, 2005

Answers to summary questions

Only numerical solutions are given.

1

4 Using $I = P/V = 4.4$ A. Select the next largest fuse value (5 A).

3

2   a   10 kΩ ± 5%
     b   The range is 10000 Ω ± 500 = (9500 Ω to 10 500 Ω).

3   a   270 kΩ ± 5%
     b   3.9 kΩ ± 10%
     c   18 Ω ± 5%

4   a   The closest value is 2400 Ω
     b   The next highest value needed to keep the current below the maximum is 2700 Ω.

5   a   2.7k Ω ± 10% = (2700 Ω ± 270 Ω)
     b   82 Ω ± 5% = (82 Ω ± 4.1 Ω)
     c   2.2 MΩ ± 5% = (2 200 000 Ω ± 110 000 Ω)

6 The largest power rating available from the list which is above 0.3 W is 0.5 W ($\frac{1}{2}$ W).

7   a $V_F = 1.8$ V

         $I_{Ftyp} = 20$ mA

     b   20 mA
     c   13.2 V, 660 Ω
     d   680 Ω

4

3

E	F	G	H
0	0	1	0
0	1	0	1
1	0	1	0
1	1	0	0

J	K	L	M	N	Q
0	0	0	1	0	1
0	0	1	1	1	0
0	1	0	1	1	0
0	1	1	1	1	0
1	0	0	0	0	1
1	0	1	0	1	1
1	1	0	0	1	1
1	1	1	0	1	1

5

2   a   0.67 A

3   c $I = 0.25$ A. Choose a relay with contacts that could handle slightly more than this – 0.5A.

6

2   a $R = 363\,636$ Ω or 363 kΩ
     b   Make R a variable resistor. Suitable value 500 kΩ

3   a $R = 6 \times 10^3$ Ω or 6 kΩ
     b   Nearest preferred value to this is 6.2 kΩ. This will give a time period of 68.2 ms.

7

2 $T = 6.67 \times 10^{-3}$ or 6.67 ms

3 $T = 0.08$s; $f = 12.5$ Hz

5   a   8 ms
     b   125 Hz
     c   0.6 V
     d   A sine (sinusoidal) wave.

8

5   a   i   36 kΩ   ii   28 kΩ
     b R_1 is the thermistor, and R_2 is the 33 kΩ resistor.

         At 0 °C: $V_{out} = 7.17$ V

         At 2 °C: $V_{out} = 8.11$ V

6   c   6 V   d   6 V   e   164 kΩ.

10

2   a   6 W   b   7 kHz

11

2   a   16.8 V

3   a   7.7 V   b   7 V

Useful information for GCSE Electronics

■ Prefixes

Electronics uses very large and very small numbers. Instead of writing lots of zeros, we use prefixes to show the number of zeros. The prefix is a symbol before the unit that tells you about the size of the number. Using prefixes means people are less likely to read the number incorrectly and can write values on circuit diagrams.

Some people like to write their number in scientific notation, particularly when using electronic calculators.

Example

3.3 MHz = 3.3 × 1 000 000 Hz = 3 300 000 Hz or 3.3×10^6 Hz.

470 nF = 470 ÷ 1 000 000 000 F = 0.00000047 F

prefix	name	number	scientific notation
T	tera	× 1 000 000 000 000	$\times 10^{12}$
G	giga	× 1 000 000 000	$\times 10^{9}$
M	mega	× 1 000 000	$\times 10^{6}$
k	kilo	× 1 000	$\times 10^{3}$
m	milli	× 0.001 (÷ 1 000)	$\times 10^{-3}$
μ	micro	× 0.000 001 (÷ 1 000 000)	$\times 10^{-6}$
n	nano	× 0.000 000 001 (÷ 1 000 000 000)	$\times 10^{-9}$
p	pico	× 0.000 000 000 001 (÷ 1 000 000 000 000)	$\times 10^{-12}$

The symbol for micro is the Greek letter mu which looks a bit like a u with a tail at the start.

All prefixes for small numbers use lowercase letters and most prefixes for large numbers use capital letters, the only exception is k. Be careful not to confuse mega and milli by carefully using a capital or lowercase letter.

You need to know what each prefix means and also how to use them.

■ More useful information

power	amplifiers
power = voltage × current; $P = VI$	voltage gain, $G_v = \dfrac{V_{out}}{V_{in}}$

Resistor colour code

The colours in the resistor colour code correspond to the following values.

BLACK	0	YELLOW	4	GREY	8
BROWN	1	GREEN	5	WHITE	9
RED	2	BLUE	6		
ORANGE	3	VIOLET	7		

The fourth band colour gives the tolerance
GOLD ± 5%   SILVER ± 10%   No fourth band ± 20%

Resistor printed code (BS 1852)

R means × 1   K means × 1 000   M means × 1 000 000
Position of the letter gives the decimal point.

Tolerances are indicated by adding a letter at the end.
J ± 5%   K ± 10%   M ± 20%
e.g. 5K6J = ± 5.6 kΩ ± 5%

Preferred values for resistors (E24 SERIES)

1.0, 1.1, 1.2, 1.3, 1.5, 1.6, 1.8, 2.0, 2.2, 2.4, 2.7, 3.0,
3.3, 3.6, 3.9, 4.3, 4.7, 5.1, 5.6, 6.2, 6.8, 7.5, 8.2, 9.1
and multiples of ten.

Resistance

$$R = \frac{\text{Voltage}}{\text{Current}} = \frac{V}{I}$$

Effective resistance, R, of up to four resistors in series is given by
$R = R_1 + R_2 + R_3 + R_4$

Effective resistance, R, of two resistors in parallel is given by $\frac{1}{R} = \frac{1}{R_1} + \frac{1}{R_2}$

ac waveforms

1 Frequency of waveform = $\frac{1}{\text{Time period}}$; $f = \frac{1}{T}$

2 peak value = 1.4 × rms value

astable and monostable generators using 555 timers

1 Monostable mode, time period $T = 1.1 R_1 \times C_1$

2 Astable mode, time period $T = \frac{(R_1 + 2R_2)C_1}{1.44}$

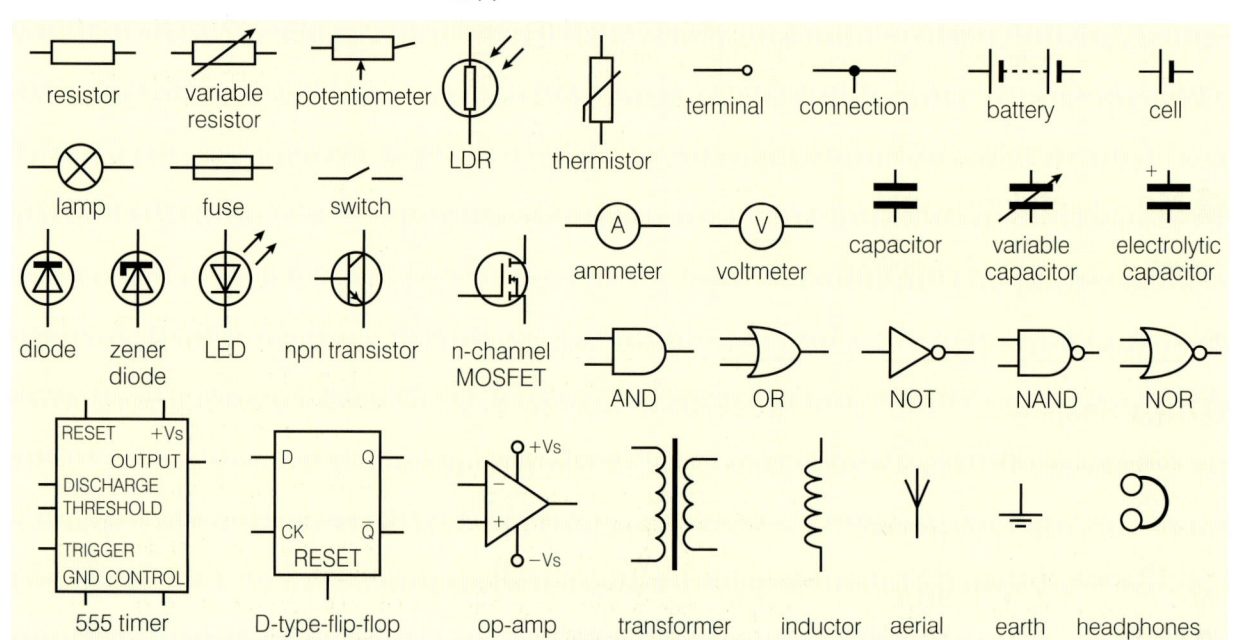

Glossary

555: the 555 timer integrated circuit.

A

ac: alternating current – made to constantly change value and direction by the applied alternating voltage.

ADC: analogue-to-digital converter. A device which converts an analogue signal to a digital one.

Aerial: a wire used to change electrical energy into electromagnetic waves if transmitting, or vice versa if receiving.

Amplitude: the maximum displacement of a wave.

Amplitude modulation: the act of changing the size of the wave to encode the information.

Analogue signal: signal that can have any value between certain set limits or a signal that can take up voltage values over a continuous range.

Astable: a circuit which generates a continuous on/off signal or pulse train.

Audio frequency: the wave frequency that is associated with sound and lies in the range of 20 Hz to 20 kHz.

B

Bandwidth: the range of frequencies where the power gain is at least half the maximum gain.

Base: one of the three terminals of the BJT.

Base resistor: the resistor that connects between the signal to be amplified and the base of the BJT.

BJT: stands for Bipolar Junction Transistor.

Breadboard: a solderless and reusable plastic base on which circuits can be quickly developed and tested.

C

Capacitor: a component which stores electrical charge.

Carrier wave: the radio wave used to transport information.

Circuit breaker: usually an electromagnetic or thermal device that stops current flowing in a circuit because of a fault.

Collector: one of the three terminals of the BJT.

Comparator: a circuit that compares two signals.

Current: the quantity of electrical charge flowing per second through a point in a circuit.

Current gain: the amount by which the signal is amplified.

D

dc power supply: a power supply which produces direct current (a current that flows in one direction only).

dc: direct current – made to flow with a constant value in a fixed direction by an applied fixed voltage.

Demodulator: strips away the RF to leave just AF.

Digital multimeter (DMM): a meter that allows you to switch to different modes to take voltage, current and resistance measurements using different ranges on the same meter.

Digital: a signal that can only have two values, high or low.

Drain: one of the three terminals of the MOSFET.

D-type flip-flop: an electronic component used to make a data latch.

E

E24 series: a range of 24 numbers and their ×10 multipliers that represent the values that resistors can have.

Electric shock: the effect on nerves, organs and tissue due to the passage of electrical current through the body.

Electrolytic capacitor: a polarised capacitor.

Emitter: one of the three terminals of the BJT.

F

Farad: the unit of capacitance.

Fibrillation: stimulation of the heart muscles that overrides the natural rhythm.

Flowchart diagram: a diagram which uses special shapes and arrows to describe a program or other process in a sequence of instructions.

Forward bias: applying the voltage across a diode in such a way that the diode is able to conduct.

Frequency: the rate at which a periodic signal repeats – expressed in Hz. Can also be defined as the number of complete waves passing through a point each second.

Frequency modulation: the act of changing the number of waves per second to encode the information.

Full-wave rectifier: a circuit containing a number of diodes (diode bridge) used to make both halves of the ac cycle become positive.

Fuse: a common type of circuit breaker that contains a thin wire that melts to break the circuit when excess current flows.

G

Gate: one of the three terminals of the MOSFET.

H

Half-wave rectifier: a circuit containing a diode used to block out the negative half of the ac cycle.

High voltage: represents 1.

I

ICs: integrated circuits.

Ideal op-amp: an op-amp with a gain of infinity (∞).

Input: the information going into a system to provide it with its 'raw materials'.

Input transducer: a transducer that converts a quantity into an electrical signal.

Inverting input: the (−) input of an op-amp.

L

LDR (Light-dependant resistor): a sensing device whose resistance changes with light level.

Light-emitting diode (LED): a component that only conducts in one direction and gives out light.

Logic gate: a component that combines digital signals.

Loudspeaker: a transducer that converts an electrical signal into sounds.

Low voltage: (usually 0 V) represents 0.

Glossary

M

Microcontroller: computers on a single IC complete with memory and all the circuits needed for input and output.

Modulation: the act of changing a property of the carrier wave to encode information onto it.

Monostable: the technical name for the 555 time delay circuit.

MOSFET: stands for Metal Oxide Semiconductor Field Effect Transistor.

N

Negative temperature coefficient (NTC): a characteristic of the thermistor, where its resistance reduces as the temperature increases.

Non-inverting input: the (+) input of an op-amp.

O

Off time: the time for which a periodic signal is low.

Ohm(Ω): the unit of resistance.

Ohm's law: the current through a resistor at a constant temperature is directly proportional to the potential difference across the resistor: $\left(I = \frac{V}{R}\right)$.

On time: the time for which a periodic signal is high.

Op-amp: operational amplifier (a general purpose, high gain amplifier chip).

Oscilloscope: an instrument that will display the picture of a changing signal.

Output: the information coming out of a system that performs the required task.

Output transducer: a transducer that converts an electrical signal into some other quantity.

P

PAT: Portable Appliance Testing.

Peak value: the maximum positive or maximum negative value that an ac supply achieves.

Polarised: has a (+) and (−) connection.

Power rating: the energy per second that the component is able to safely develop without suffering damage.

Printed code: a means of using figures and letters to represent the value of a resistor.

Process: what is done to the inputs in order to create the outputs.

Program: sequence of instructions that a computer can interpret and carry out.

Protection diode: a diode connected across the transducer to protect the transistor from being damaged by the high voltage surge when the transistor switches off.

Pulse generator: a common name for the astable.

Pulse: a signal which goes high for a certain time and then goes low again; a pulse train is a continuous stream of pulses.

R

Radio communication: the means by which information is sent over a distance using radio waves.

Radio frequency: the part of the electromagnetic spectrum used for radio communication.

RC circuit: a capacitor and a resistor connected together and used to produce time delays.

Relay: an electromechanical switch.

Resistor colour code: the system of coloured rings used on resistors to indicate their values in ohms.

Resistor: a component that controls the flow of current in a circuit.

Reverse bias: applying a voltage across a diode in such a way that it will block the flow of current.

Rising edge: when a digital signal changes from a low to a high.

Risk assessment: taking into account possible dangers and modifying your actions so that you work safely.

Root mean square (rms): the equivalent steady value that would provide the same power as the ac supply.

S

Saturated: the output of the op-amp is at the + supply or at 0 V.

Selectivity: the ability of a radio receiver to distinguish between two radio stations that transmit on frequencies close together.

Sensitivity: the ability of a radio receiver to receive a weak signal from a distant station.

Smoothing capacitor: a large-value capacitor used as a storage reservoir that acts to reduce the fluctuation (ripple) of the rectified signal.

Source: one of the three terminals of the MOSFET.

SPNO: (Single Pole, Normally Open) one of the common arrangements of relay contacts.

Subsystem: an individual input, process or output within a system.

Switch: a device used to connect and disconnect a circuit.

System: a collection of inputs, processes and outputs that together perform a task.

T

Thermistor: a sensing device whose resistance changes with temperature.

Timebase: the number of seconds each cm represents across the oscilloscope screen.

Tolerance: the acceptable error range due to the manufacturing and construction technique in the value of the resistor.

Transducer: a component which changes energy from one form to another.

Transducer driver: a circuit that 'boosts' or amplifies a signal so that it can operate a transducer.

Transformer: a device used to change the value of an ac supply. It can be used to step the voltage up or down.

Transistor: a component that boosts a signal.

Trigger: the signal (and the name of the pin) that starts the 555 timing period.

Truth table: a table that shows all the possible inputs and outputs of a logic circuit.

V

Variable resistor: a resistor whose value can be changed or adjusted.

Vertical sensitivity (Y-sensitivity): the number of volts that are needed to move the oscilloscope trace up by 1 cm.

Voltage (potential difference or pd): the difference in energy levels in a circuit that causes the current to flow.

Voltage divider: a circuit which uses two resistors to divide a voltage into two smaller voltages.

Voltage gain: ratio of amplifier output voltage to amplifier input voltage.

W

Working voltage: the maximum voltage that a capacitor can withstand.

Index

Key terms, and page(s) where defined, appear in blue type.

4017 chip 65–7
555 chip 50–2, 55–6, 60, 62
556 chip 52

A

ac (alternating current) 87
  conversion to dc 88–91
  safety 9
accident prevention 11–13
ADC 76, 101
aerial 95
AF amplifier 96
alarm systems 18
AM see amplitude modulation
alternating current see ac
amplifiers 84–6, 96
amplitude 61, 85
amplitude modulation 93–4, 93
  transmission 97
analogue signals 73, 93, 101
analogue-to-digital converter (ADC) 76
AND gate 32
astable circuit 56-8, 56
audio amplifiers 84–5
audio frequency 93

B

bandwidth 85
base 39, 40
base resistor 40
batteries 14
BJT 38, 39, 41
breadboards 21, 21-3
burns 8

C

capacitance 47
capacitors 46–9, 46
  electrolytic 48
  in rectifier circuits 91
carrier wave 93
cathode ray tube 60
cells 14
circuit breakers 12–13, 12
clocks 54
coaxial cable 85
collector 39

comparator circuits 16, 73, 76
  light sensor 77
  op amps 74–5
  porch light 80
  temperature 81–2
continuous pulses 55
  applications 54
controlled assessment
  basics 104
  design 105–6
  planning 107–9
counting circuits 65–8
current 27
current gain 38

D

D-type flip-flop 69–70, 69
DAB radio 98
DAC 101
dc (direct current) 87
  safety 8
dc power supply 21
deflection plates 61
demodulator 95
digital-analogue converter (DAC) 101
digital circuits 30–1
  logic gates 32–7
digital multimeter (DMM) 22
digital signals 30, 101
direct current see dc
drain terminal 40

E

E24 series resistors 24, 25
electric shock 9
electrolytic capacitor 48
emitter 39
explosions 8, 9

F

falling edge triggering 51
farad 46, 47
fault finding 23
fibrillation 9
fire 9
firmware 100
first aid 9
flash memory 100
floating output 31
flowchart diagrams 102

FM (frequency modulation) 93, 94, 97–8
frequency 55, 61, 85
frequency divider 70–1
frequency modulation (FM) 93, 94, 97–8
full-wave rectifier 89
fuses 11

G

gain 74
gate terminal 40

H

half-wave rectifier 89
hertz 55
high voltage circuits 9
high voltage (digital) 30

I

IC (integrated circuit) 34
  555 chip 50–2
ideal op-amp 74
input (to a system) 14, 16, 18
input transducer 15, 16, 18
integrated circuits 34
inverting input 74

K

Kilby, Jack 34

L

latches 69–71
LDR (light-dependent resistor) 77, 80
light-emitting diode (LED) 14, 22, 27–8
logic circuits 36
logic gates 30, 32–7
loudspeakers 59, 96
low voltage (digital) 30

M

mains circuits 10
  safety 11
  see also ac
mains plug 10
microcontroller 17, 100
modulation 93
monostable 51
MOSFET 38, 40–1

Index

N
NAND gate 33
negative coefficient 70
negative temperature coefficient 81
noise 85
non-inverting input 74
NOR gate 33
NOT gate 32
Noyce, Robert 34

O
off time 55
ohm 24
Ohm's law 27, 28, 78
on time 55
op-amp 74, 74–6
OR gate 32
oscilloscope 59, 60–1
output (of a system) 14, 16, 18
output transducer 15, 16, 18, 59

P
PAT (portable appliance testing) 11
peak value 87
periodic signals 55
 generation 56–7
polarisation 48
power amplifiers 44
power rating 26
power supplies 8, 21
processes (of a system) 16
program 100, 102
printed code 26
protection diode 40
pulse 55
pulse generator 56-8, **56**

R
radio communication 93
 signal encoding 93–4
 transmission 97–8
radio frequency 93
radio receiver 93, 95-6
radio spectrum 97
RC **circuits 48**
rectifier circuits 88–91
regulator 81, 91
relay 42
research 108
resistors 22
 colour coding 24–5, **24**
 E24 series 25
 power rating 24
 thermistor 81
 variable 78
reverse bias 27
RF tuned circuit 95
rising edge 65
risk assessment 11
root mean square 87

S
safety 8–9
 accident prevention 11–13
 mains electricity 11–12
saturation 74, 75
selectivity 96
sensitivity 96
sequences 67–8
smoothing capacitor 81
source terminal 40
SPNO relay 42, 43
stored charge 9
subsystems 15

T
terminal boxes 102
thermistor 81
time constant 49
time delay circuits 49, 50–2
time period 55
timebase 61
tolerance 24, 26
traffic lights 67–8
transducer 16, **95**
 output 59
transducer driver 16, 38–9, **38**
 relay switches 42–3
transducer 15
transformer 88, **89**
transistor 38–41, **38**
 see also BJT, MOSFET
trigger signal 51
truth tables 32–3, **32**, 35, 37–8

switches 30–1, **30**
 relay 42
system diagrams 14, 15, 16–17, 19, 108
systems 14
 design 18–19
 inputs and outputs 15–17

V
variable resistor 78
vertical sensitivity 61
voltage 24
voltage divider 78–9
voltage gain 75, **84**
voltage regulator 91

W
working voltage 46